The Management Delusion

Matt Casey

CONTENTS

CONTENTS

1

INTRODUCTION

"I choose a lazy person to do a hard job. Because a lazy person will find an easy way to do it"

Bill Gates

Managers are usually hard workers. That's how they get promoted. It's why they get put in charge. But hard workers tend to try to solve problems with hard work, so over the years these hard workers took on more and more responsibility, and the management role became increasingly bloated. It's now reached a point where what we expect of our managers is completely out of balance with what most of them are capable of. The job is too hard now, and as a result most of us have had far more bad managers than good ones. That's a disaster. The role is too important for that kind of failure rate. Imagine if we'd had more bad pilots than good ones.

It wasn't supposed to be like this.

The working world the manager was created for was a far simpler place than the one it functions in today. At first, a manager pretty much only needed to be scary. There was no employee engagement, no career development, no servant leadership or performance coaching. It was just a scary guy screaming the dreams out of a group of people with low expectations and nowhere else to go. That scary guy didn't have to do anything particularly difficult to get people to do the work he wanted them to do. He just pointed them to their spot on the factory floor and said "stand there and do this as many times as you can before you die". That was being a manager.

That isn't the job now. We can't just be scary. In fact, modern managers must be all things to all people. We must be inspirational, authoritative and organised. We must be inventive, emotionally intelligent, patient and calm. We must be bold, but cautious. We must drive change, but maintain order. We must be selfless, but demanding. And we must be all of these things consistently, because the moment we make a mistake pretty much everyone hates us and loads of stuff goes wrong.

Take a moment to think about the personality traits and skills necessary to consistently be all of those things. I don't know anyone who is this person. I'm pretty sure nobody is this person. In fact, I believe that if you were to ever meet this person you would know immediately, because they would physically glow. Captain America is this person. Nobody else. But in most organisations today, roughly one in seven employees perform management duties. One in seven. We are organising ourselves in such a way that success depends on one in seven people being better than the best person we've ever met, and then we're surprised when everything is horrible. An entire career of working with and training managers at every level has proved to me beyond doubt that far fewer than one in seven people are capable of doing this job. It's not even close to that. Have you met people? Most of them are dreadful.

The failure of this approach has been obvious for a long time. Employee engagement studies consistently paint a horrible picture of a workforce who are disinterested in their jobs and distrustful of their managers, and this has been the case for several years with barely any sign of improvement. Almost universally, our attempts to address this problem have centered around spending more and more time and money on trying to improve the managers. We keep trying to make the managers better so they can meet the new demands we place on them. But we keep failing, and the demands keep increasing. What if we're going about it all wrong? What if instead of trying to make the managers better, we should be trying to make management easier?

That's why I'm writing this book. A few years ago I stepped back from my near religious belief in management and instead of asking myself how I could be better at it, I asked myself how I could make it easy enough that I couldn't mess it up. The result was what I have come to refer to as Minimum Effective Management. This is the absolute minimum amount of management I need to carry out in order to generate the outcomes I want. Working this way has allowed me to create workplaces that everybody can thrive in without the need for superhuman managers whose decisions determine the working lives of everyone else. It's a way of working that any manager can adopt without needing to learn a single new skill.

I believe management is important. What we do affects the lives of other people in real and significant ways, both in and out of work. And we are failing those people far too often. But it's not our fault, the job is just too hard now. Unless it's made significantly simpler, this will always be the case. The approach of trying to improve the managers has failed, because the standard required is unrealistic. What I've discovered is that almost anyone can be a great manager, as long as they don't try to take on the ridiculous level of responsibility we have come to believe the role demands. We've been adding new structures to the old foundations of management for decades, when what we really need to do is rip it down and rebuild it from scratch based on the requirements and capabilities of today's working world.

So that's what I did. I've tried to avoid making this book an instruction manual. I hope that I explain the approach and how I implement it in a way that's digestible, but it's not a step by step guide. I'm not trying to tell anyone what they should or shouldn't be doing - just what I do, and perhaps more importantly, what I don't do.

This is how I achieve everything traditional management claims it will achieve but consistently fails to. This is the approach I use to be successful without ever feeling pressured, working crazy hours, or dealing with the hassle and stress that managers routinely face.

This is the easy way to do a hard job.

2

WHY IT'S NOT WORKING

Management has been failing for a long time now. Employee engagement has been appalling for years and has shown little sign of improvement. Global productivity is in decline. At the time of writing, Gallup have just released their latest State of the Global Workplace report[1], which shows that a shocking 85% of global employees are disengaged with their work. 18% reported being actively disengaged. Take a moment to think about that. The purpose of management is to engage employees. That's it. We don't do anything ourselves, all our results are achieved through the actions of our employees. But only 15% of those employees even care about their job, and nearly 20% of them are so unhappy with it that they are actively trying to do it badly.

The question we have to ask ourselves isn't if

---

[1] State of the Global Workplace, Gallup,
https://www.gallup.com/workplace/238079/state-global-workplace.aspx

management is working or not. That question has been answered emphatically: it isn't. Management is arguably the function most crucial to the success of any business, but we are accepting a failure rate from it that we wouldn't from any other role. And that failure rate clearly demonstrates that it cannot be the fault of the managers themselves. If 85% of planes crashed, we would immediately recognise there was a problem with those planes. We wouldn't blame the pilots.

"Hey Dave, what happened to that plane full of people brimming with hope for the future?"

"Oh, it's in a million pieces at the bottom of the sea, Diane"

"Another one!? These pilots are rubbish aren't they...when's the next one taking off?"

We obviously wouldn't blame the pilots, we'd fix the planes. Immediately. We wouldn't even contemplate letting another one into the sky. And when it comes to our organisations, the managers are our pilots. They're the people responsible for what happens to everyone we place in their charge. Management is the plane we give them. And it keeps crashing.

The reason for this is that management itself is an unsuitable vehicle to deliver the things people want from work. It has been incredibly clear what those things are for years now. They've been explained to us a thousand times before. Almost universally, whenever anyone has sought to find out why so many employees are disengaged and why productivity is so disappointing, what they've found is that people want things out of their work that they're just not getting. The central pillars of what keeps an employee engaged and motivated have changed. Arguably these used to be job security and reward, but this is no longer the case. Today, people have been found to want different things from their work, and I'd be amazed if this was news to you. Almost every manager I have ever spoken to has known what people really want from work now:

- **Autonomy** - People have become less comfortable with the idea of having a 'boss'. They want a manager who supports them and whom they respect, but they don't want to be told what to do

- **Purpose** - People want to know why they're doing what they're doing, and they want to see the effect their work has. They don't want a meaningless list of tasks they have to perform. They want to be part of achieving something real that they believe in

- **Growth** - People want to use and develop their skills, and this is more important to them than financial reward. Reward is still important, but people want their increased reward to be a result of their increased value. They want to grow and be rewarded for that growth

- **Recognition** - People live their lives in public now, and they compare themselves to each other. Recognition has always been important, but perhaps now more than ever

I'm sure none of this is new information to anyone at this point. We know all of this, and we've known it for long enough that if management was capable of consistently providing it, it would have done so by now. I've been hearing about the importance of providing these things for at least a decade. I have read several management books that talk about their importance at great length. I've met very few managers who don't recognise that providing these things to their staff is crucial. Yet despite all of this, nothing seems more common to me than a manager who knows the importance of these things, but who is managing people in exactly the same way they have always been managed. It's like we think that simply wanting a different outcome from the same management activities will be enough to create it. I frequently hear people espouse the importance of providing these things to our employees, but rarely hear anyone actually explain how to do it. It's like we're being told again and again: "When you make a cake, it should be delicious", but nobody is giving us a clue how to actually make a delicious cake. I know a cake should be delicious, that doesn't mean I can bake. Similarly, we pretty much all know what people want from work now, but that hasn't led to us being able to deliver it to them. Instead, we seem to have acknowledged that our employees want a totally different outcome, and have then proceeded to behave in exactly the same way.

To unpack the reasons for that, consider what these requirements - Autonomy, Purpose, Growth, and Recognition - are for a moment. Notice that these not only weren't requirements back when the management role was created, they would in fact have been laughable requirements at that time. The role was actually created to provide almost the exact opposite of these things. We've ended up retrofitting it in an attempt to make it do something it was never designed to do, and in many cases our role as the manager actively incentivises us to behave in ways that stop this kind of workplace emerging.

I think this is the reason we haven't been able to adapt to the new needs workers have despite knowing full well what they are. The management role was designed to deliver the opposite of this workplace, and despite our best efforts it simply isn't suitable to deliver it as it stands. Management itself is working against us in our bid to give our employees the things they want and need from work.

THAT'S MUCH HOTTER WATER

We're a boiling frog

In case you're unfamiliar with the fable, it goes like this: A frog is placed in a pot of extremely hot water, and quickly jumps out on account of not wanting to die. That same frog is then placed in tepid water, where it's perfectly comfortable and stays put. The water is then slowly brought to the boil, but the frog doesn't notice the water getting hotter and is eventually boiled to death without ever even trying to get out.

The message is that we don't tend to notice or react to gradual change. This is what has happened to us with management. The pot the management frog is sitting in is nothing like the pot it was initially placed into. But the change didn't happen suddenly.

The job started as a relatively simple one, and with no viable alternative. There was no internet, no cloud, and no instantaneous way to organise large groups of people or move information around. The only way to achieve those things was through a hierarchical structure. So that's what we used. We put in a structure of managers who told people what to do, and who told each other what was going on in their little slice of the org chart. They didn't really have much else to do other than command, control and report. But once those managers were in place, when each new requirement at work emerged - whether it was from the employer or the employees - it invariably fell to those managers to deliver it.

Coaching? The managers will do it.

Employee engagement? The managers will do it.

Salary reviews? The managers will do it.

Personal development? The managers will do it.

Forecasting? The managers will do it.

Team building? The managers will do it.

Goal setting? The managers will do it.

Performance reviews? The managers will do it.

On and on it went, and slowly but surely we transformed what was once a simple role into something so complex that it's now incredibly rare to find anyone who can do all of it to the standard required. I believe that if we were organising a company today and we'd never heard of management, there is no way that we would choose the same solution. We wouldn't expect a single person to deliver all the things a manager delivers to small silos of people. Instead, we would use technology to spread those responsibilities around, and we'd ensure our natural leaders would have time and space to lead without being buried in management admin.

The way we've approached meeting the new requirements has had a twofold impact. As the demands on managers have grown, this has in turn led to each manager being able to manage fewer people. Obviously the more you have to do for each person, the fewer people you will have time to manage. This in turn has meant that we need more managers. If we have 40 employees and a manager who can manage up to 40 people, we will only need one manager. But if the management role is so complex that a manager can only manage say, five people, then all of a sudden we will need at least ten managers across three layers of management. And the more managers we have in an organisation, the more complicated the management role tends to become as they have to organise themselves around one another. This takes up even more of the managers time, and lowers the number of people they can effectively manage even further. It's a problem that grows exponentially.

As a result, even small businesses today often have multiple layers of management that give birth to complex organisational problems. The more things managers have to do, the fewer people they can manage, and the more managers we need. This is no longer an easy job that very few people need to perform. It's now an extremely difficult job that lots of people need to perform.

That's very different. That's much hotter water. If someone put us in this pot, we'd get out of it immediately. But because we've just been sitting in it as it has heated up, we're still here. Imagine for a moment that you'd never heard of management, and you asked someone to organise a company for you. If they came back to you and said, "So this is my plan: we'll basically ignore the internet, and then one person in seven will spend half their time monitoring the other six, and the other half of their time sitting in meeting rooms inventing new transitive verbs", I think there's a good chance you'd punch that person in the throat. It would be a ridiculous way to organise a company today, given all the tools we have available.

I THINK MANAGERS HAVE DIRTY HANDS

Conformity of thought

Throughout my career, I've been lucky enough to spend a fairly significant amount of time with accountants.

Now now, don't be jealous. It's unbecoming.

During this joyous time, I came to notice a pattern to how they would use one of their primary tools - Excel. They often didn't know what it could really do. They all understood the same key set of features that allowed them to get their job done, but very few of them had ever scratched at that surface and found all the things it could do that would have enabled them to get it done faster. They had never tried to find an easier way to do their job.

The fact I was aware of these things and they weren't wasn't due to any superior intellect on my part. I wasn't any smarter or more capable than they were. It was just that I had actually looked for these things, and I had looked for them because we had a totally different way of approaching problems. Because I'm not an accountant.

To be a good accountant, you need specific traits. Your brain needs to approach things in a certain way. You need to be organised, diligent, methodical and have incredible attention to detail. These are all traits I don't have. I could never be an accountant, because my brain works completely differently. In fact, my total lack of those traits forces me to get inventive when I'm faced with situations that require them. Early in my career I had a job that involved maintaining an Excel spreadsheet, and I used to constantly make small mistakes because my attention to detail is extremely poor. Instead of attempting to address this weakness that I'd always had, I tried to identify features within Excel that would negate it. As a result, I found things it could do that most accountants would never even have looked for. They wouldn't have needed to. They could have just done the work correctly in the first place.

The traits that lead to someone becoming an accountant are generally mutually exclusive to the traits that would lead someone to solve the problems the way I did. And because all accountants need those traits, they all pretty much use Excel the same way.

This is true of almost every job. There are consistent and identifiable patterns to the way people who end up in certain jobs approach solving problems, which means there are consistent and identifiable patterns to the way those jobs end up being performed. So, with that in mind, how do we think a person who has been attracted to a role that gives them control and authority would approach solving most problems?

With control and authority.

When a manager considers how to solve a problem, most of them are going to reach straight for those tools. As a result, most of our management solutions are based around a manager exerting control or authority over a situation or person. That does not mean those are the only tools that could achieve the desired result, or even that they're the best tools for it. It simply means they're the tools the people we're asking to solve the problems are most comfortable using. But when we solve problems using these tools we're actively working against creating the kind of workplaces that employees now want.

This conformity of thought feeds itself. When a manager is in a position to hire someone else for a management role, they will obviously look for the qualities they believe a manager should possess. And those qualities will almost certainly be the qualities they themselves possess. What this has led to is the management role often being the least diverse role in any given business. Most managers pretty much think exactly the same way, because they were chosen for the role by other managers. Those managers naturally chose people like themselves, because to do anything else would be to suggest they themselves weren't suitable for the role.

The solutions these incredibly similar managers have implemented are usually based around the behavioural traits and instincts of people who lean towards control and authority. On the rare occasions that a manager thinks differently and suggests an approach that doesn't rely on those things, they tend to find themselves coming up against a common logical fallacy: the appeal to a common practice.

The appeal to a common practice is a flawed argument that simply says, "what you think is wrong, because everybody else thinks something different". It ignores the validity of the argument itself, and simply dismisses it without consideration, purely on the grounds that nobody else thinks it. A sad example of someone running into this problem can be found in the 19th century, with Dr Ignaz

Semmelweis. Now known as 'the saviour of mothers', Semmelweis noticed that the incidences of an often fatal illness known as childbed fever could be drastically reduced if doctors simply disinfected their hands between seeing patients. Although he was able to consistently demonstrate this to be true, he wasn't able to explain why it was true, and as it went against the accepted medical opinions of the time, he was ignored. Not just ignored in fact, he was mocked for making the claim at all, and his career was ruined. Other doctors didn't like the implication that they were causing harm, rather than preventing it. The frustration of this contributed to Semmelweis suffering a nervous breakdown and being committed to an asylum, where he was swiftly beaten to death by the guards. Yep, the world is horrible.

At the risk of suffering the 21st Century equivalent, and with a far less noble cause - I think managers have dirty hands. A lot of what we do, although well-intentioned, actually generates bad outcomes, and I think because most of us were chosen for our role based on having the same traits, we rarely come up with anything different.

NOBODY CAN GIVE THAT TO YOU

IT'S ALREADY YOURS

We swallow the fly

There was an old lady who swallowed a bird
How absurd to swallow a bird!
She swallowed the bird to catch the spider
She swallowed the spider to catch the fly
I don't know why she swallowed a fly - perhaps she'll die

A lot of the activities we have to carry out as managers are only necessary because we took an earlier action in an attempt to manage something else. We have a tendency to solve one problem whilst creating several new ones that are harder to solve - like a cleaner with muddy shoes walking around the house doing some light dusting.

When you find a great manager, you'll often find that it's what they don't do that makes them great. Have you ever spoken to someone who loves their manager, and asked them why? I can almost guarantee that you heard the words "lets me" again and again.

"She just lets me get on with it"

"He lets me make mistakes"

"He lets me work the way I want to work"

"She lets me be myself"

"She lets me make my own decisions"

People crave autonomy and freedom, but almost by definition the management role takes most of this away. We typically get praised for giving back something that was theirs to begin with. We shouldn't ever have to give our employees responsibility for their actions, because that responsibility is inalienable. Nobody can give that to you, because it's already yours, you had that the moment you became an adult. Management takes responsibility away, then gets praise for giving it back. Like when my dog steals another dog's ball, then expects a treat for letting it go.

Management in its current form is often an exercise in undoing problems that management itself created. Often when we're solving a problem, that problem is of our own making.

WE HAVE GIVEN THE MANAGER TOO MANY INTERESTS TO REPRESENT

We have to direct the trolley

The Trolley Problem is a famous thought experiment that provides us with an ethical dilemma. There are a number of different variations, a simple one is as follows:

There is a runaway trolley heading down some railway tracks, across which five people are tied up and unable to escape. You are standing next to a lever which would allow you to redirect the trolley to a side track, saving the lives of those five people. However, there are two people tied across that side track. You have two options:

- Do nothing and allow the trolley to kill the five people on the main track

- Pull the lever and divert the trolley onto the side track where it will kill two people who would have otherwise survived

What should you do?

Now, obviously the situation itself is one you're unlikely to actually find yourself in unless you upset the guy from the Saw movies, or you get a little bit too carried away with a particularly niche role playing fetish. However, the essence of the problem can be felt in a huge number of the decisions a leader has to make. I'm writing this book at the time of the Covid crisis, and our governments happen to be facing a trolley problem right now. Any action, or inaction, on their part will almost certainly result in people dying. But it will be different people depending on their choices. Too little caution and more people will die due to the pandemic. Too much caution and more people will die due to the lockdowns. This is the trolley problem on a global scale. Hopefully by the time you're reading this everything will have sorted itself out, but if not...hello from the Before Times, we used to have a delicious thing called an apple, and we were allowed outside. It was excellent.

Although the trolley problems managers face aren't anywhere near as significant as the one our governments are facing right now, they are still disruptive and often have consequences that make our jobs much harder. The root of the problem is that we always have the interests of several different parties to consider - the company's, all of our employees', and our own. Often, we find ourselves in situations where any of the following will be true:

- Doing what's best for the company will not be what's best for our employees

- Doing what's best for our employees will not be what's best for us

- Doing what's best for one of our employees will not be what's best for another

We have given the manager too many interests to represent, and this isn't good for any of the parties involved. It leads to bad results for everyone. Every manager I know has several stories of times they've had to make a decision where no matter which choice they made, one of the interests they were supposed to represent would be worse off for it. In these situations, their personal biases and incentives often meant that the decisions they ended up making were not necessarily the ones they objectively believed to be the best all round.

This is not to say that managers shouldn't be making tough choices - they have to be made and it's part of our job to make them. But the way we frame the management role currently means that we make those choices harder, and the fallout from those choices greater.

As I will show later on, by simply reframing what our employees think we're responsible for in terms of their career, their reward, and how they work, we can remove most of these situations entirely.

NOTHING BAD HAPPENS IF NOTHING HAPPENS AT ALL

We build around the worst

Today, more than at any other time in my life, we seem to be terrified of making mistakes. We take a far harsher view of someone who fails as a result of making mistakes than we do of someone who fails as a result of excessive caution. When someone is extremely cautious and fails, we just think they were unfortunate in spite of their caution. But when someone takes risks and fails, we think they were reckless. As a result, managers understandably have veered towards caution. This is one of the reasons it's so difficult to create an engaged workplace with the traditional management approach. If as the manager I will be accountable for all the mistakes my team makes, it will be emotionally difficult for me to back away and give them the autonomy they need to be their best, even though I know it's what they want. If I'm going to get the blame if everything goes wrong, can you really be surprised if I find it difficult to step back and let someone else make the decisions? When managers are responsible for the outcomes, and failure as a result of action is treated as worse than failure as the result of caution, then of course they are going to be tempted to micromanage.

Taking on full responsibility for the outcomes is

something I used to think was intrinsic to being a good manager. I still remember my very first day of management training. I'd gone into the session fairly reluctantly, as at that time I had a pretty negative view of management as a whole. I'd walked in half expecting to be subjected to a series of lessons on how to trick and manipulate people that I would find abhorrent. But very early on, the trainer said something that has stayed with me ever since.

"They take the fame, you take the blame"

The sentiment of this really surprised me. Up until then, I'd always had managers that had acted completely counter to that. When things went well, they took all the credit. When things went badly, they blamed everyone else. I had zero respect for any of those managers, but I had just assumed that's what managers did. Managers were just dicks, that's what I thought. Finding out that, in fact, those people just hadn't been doing the job properly was kind of a revelation to me. If that was the wrong way to do the job, I wanted to know what the right way was. That statement was enough to make me think that maybe there was a small chance I could become a manager without having to aggressively hate myself.

That message would go on to become a cornerstone of how I managed people, and how I taught other people to manage. I too would share it on the first day of the training I would give people. But what I've come to realise is that this asks too much of the manager emotionally. If we don't get the credit for it going well, but we do get the blame for it going badly, then of course we're going to be inclined to stop things going wrong even if that comes at the expense of good outcomes.

After all, nothing bad happens if nothing happens at all.

All of this manifests itself in the most management thing of all the management things - process. Processes were always a pitfall for me. I can all too easily geek out on an elegant process, and become enamoured by the prospect of controlling every little detail. I used to want a process for everything. But over the years I've seen that most processes don't enable us to get the best outcomes. Far from it in fact, they are usually implemented to prevent the worst outcomes, and that often comes at the expense of the best ones.

Processes are very often created in response to failures, and then implemented with no thought for anything other than preventing those failures reoccurring. Imagine you have a team of people who have been given total decision making autonomy. This team has been crushing it for months. Everything has been going great, people have been making great decisions and they're all fully engaged and happy. Then one day, someone does something really stupid. Stupid enough that not only do you notice, but *your* boss notices too. And then your boss tells you to make sure it doesn't happen again. What would you do? The most likely answer is that you would implement a process that would give you more control over the decisions everyone makes. You would make sure that nobody could make that stupid mistake again, because that's what you'd been told to.

But the process you put in place would almost certainly limit some of the autonomy that had previously been making your team so successful and keeping your people so engaged. You won't just prevent that bad thing happening again, you'll prevent a lot of good things happening too.

Now, imagine a few months later someone else does a different stupid thing. Now you'll have to stop this stupid thing from happening again as well, so you'll probably do exactly what you did last time. You'll create a process. And a little bit more autonomy will be chipped away.

This is how managers end up destroying autonomy even when they want to provide it. It's how they end up taking away the opportunities people have to learn and grow through making their own decisions. They rarely make the conscious decision to do it. Nobody wants it. It's just a gradual erosion of choice, like waves hitting a beach. Each time one person makes a mistake, a manager gets the blame and creates a process and policy that is then applied to every single person to ensure nobody makes that mistake in future. Pretty soon nobody can do anything in case that thing is wrong. Nobody can think or act on their own. Imagine a group of children playing in a park, and each time one of them hurts themselves on a ride, none of the children is allowed back on that ride. It won't be long until you have a park with zero accidents, but nobody playing. Is that really succeeding?

I see this thinking everywhere. We control most of the decisions of most of our employees because we're worried about what might go wrong if we don't. We're designing our organisations for our worst people, then we're shocked when our best people don't thrive in them.

DATA OR IT DIDN'T HAPPEN

We torture the data

"If you torture the data long enough, it will confess to anything"

Ronald H. Coase

Back in the early days of social media, before it became an inexhaustible portal of rage and hate, it was often used by people to talk to each other about fun things they'd done. A phrase emerged during this time which may or may not still be in use: "Pics or it didn't happen". In other words, unless you can prove it happened, we don't believe you. It was always kind of jokey, but at the same time kind of serious. I always hated it. What it led to is something that we all just consider normal now, but that I still hate every bit as much as I did when it started; swarms of people filming everything they do to make sure they can prove to other people that they did it. The quest for proof of the experience has superseded the experience itself.

Management does the exact same thing. Management wants pics for everything.

If you can't measure it, it doesn't exist

If you can't measure it, you can't improve it

If you can't measure it, you can't manage it

The lifeblood of management is data and measurement. We have to have data so we can show the other managers what we've done. We have to have data to measure how well everyone is doing. We have to have data to see the things we must change. Data is everything. If a manager does something and there's no data, then they didn't really do it. If a manager thinks something but can't confirm it with data, then they can't act on it. It always comes down to data.

This is a huge part of why we're failing to engage people. Data isn't engaging. Somewhere along the way we have totally dismissed the human element of work and come to believe that it's possible for us to measure and control every aspect of it. It isn't. Life isn't like that. Even Tim Ferris, author of the brilliant *The 4-hour Work Week* and practically the godfather of data driven decisions, has come to realise this. As he told GQ recently, "not everything that is meaningful can be measured".

Management tries to measure everything, but a lot of these things can't really be captured or communicated with data. Imagine running an engagement survey across all your friends, or giving your husband or wife a performance review score. How do you think those activities would affect those relationships? Even if the data you gathered somehow turned out to be meaningful, accurate or even helpful, the act itself would be damaging. It implies distance. It implies disconnection. The management obsession with data drives wedges between the human relationships that need to form in order to build the kind of workplaces we all want to be part of now.

Even on the occasions where using data may be appropriate, there are huge problems with our execution. I have found that the term *data driven decisions* is so often a lie. It's a catchphrase people use to try to make themselves appear scientifically inclined, but the truth is their decisions are rarely data driven at all. For more often the opposite is the case; their data is decision driven.

A lot of the time people decide what they want to do, then torture the data until it gives them permission to do it. I don't think they always do this consciously, but they still do it. During the Covid crisis I have had several discussions with people who have the opposite view to mine on the validity of the lockdown approach - yet we have continually used the exact same data to make our totally opposite points. Data tends to just mean whatever we want it to mean.

When we use data to support a decision we've already made and probably have no genuine intention of changing, it becomes either an exercise in blame avoidance, a hoop we need to jump through, or a battering ram we use to get someone else to agree with us. There's nothing scientific or methodical about that, so if that's what we're doing, we might as well just skip the step entirely.

Strangely, the bigger problem with our use of data is the exact opposite. Often, rather than making up our mind and then making sure the data proves us right, we instead refuse to engage our minds at all and we let the data decide for us. Often we let it paralyse us, or override our critical thinking. There's so often an irrationality to the value we place on data when we use it this way. Without getting too hippyish, the human brain is the most complex thing we are aware of in the entire universe, and each human being has been feeding data into it constantly for their entire lives. When an experienced human who has been exposed to countless relevant situations reaches a conclusion on a problem they have considered, that conclusion is the result of one of the most powerful computers in the universe computing years and years of data. That should be more valuable to us than a spreadsheet completed over a couple of weeks. But we've started to dismiss all individual opinions as anecdotal, no matter whose the opinion is, and this is not sensible or productive. If we need something to be in a spreadsheet in order to ascribe any value to it, we're not being scientific. We're being lazy and irrational. But unfortunately, this has seemingly become the 'correct' way to do things. The challenge I always hear to this point is "ah, but human beings are biased". Yes, yes they are. And they bring that bias to how they interpret the spreadsheets as well. We haven't solved human bias by using data, we've just added a step.

I recently saw an incredible example of this passive surrender to the data. An article came up in my news feed proclaiming that scientists had done extensive research and confirmed that the safest height a human being could dive from is 15 meters. The article explained in great length the methodology they used, the results they gathered and their conclusion. It was very thorough, and the data was compelling. Then out of nowhere, as a complete after thought, the article stated: "The world record height for a dive is 58.8 meters". Apparently this real world thing that actually happened could be discounted in the face of their sacred data. Actually diving is a terrible way to learn about diving, it's no match for throwing a sensor covered mannequin into a swimming pool a thousand times. That 58.8 meter dive is anecdotal, it doesn't count. The data clearly shows that a dive can absolutely be no more than 15 meters, so that's the end of that. What, are you going to trust the anecdotal evidence of a thing that actually happened over our data? You Luddite.

I have worked in so many places where the time we wasted gathering the data required to make data driven decisions almost certainly exceeded the time we may have wasted by making a judgement call on what to do and being wrong a few times. And it wasn't even as if the approach was stopping us making mistakes anyway. We were still frequently getting things wrong despite following the data. This reliance on data plays into the excessively cautious way we've come to approach work, and life in general. Seemingly, nobody ever gets in trouble for spending months and months gathering data and planning without acting, but they absolutely should. Time doesn't care why it got wasted, it's still wasted. I remember having an argument with a colleague a few years ago. He'd been collecting data and calling meeting after meeting trying to plan out a fairly big piece of work. He wouldn't make a single decision until there was data to support it, and I'd become sick of it and told him it was time to just act. His response to this was to patronisingly tell me the story of the tortoise and the hare. He was of course trying to suggest that being slow and cautious is better than being fast and rash (despite that not actually being the point of the fable). So I pointed this out to him...

A hare will always beat a tortoise in a race. Always. It won't even be close. It's a stupid fable. Have you ever seen those two animals? Hare wins. Hare always wins. The hare could make a thousand mistakes, it wouldn't matter one bit.

The hare will win, because the hare moves quickly. Please, if you're ever in a situation where you can bet on the winner of a race between a tortoise and a hare, for the love of God, bet on the hare. The hare is going to win.

I didn't win that argument unfortunately. We carried on just messing about with models whilst failing miserably in the real world. I did get to see some pretty diagrams of what success would have looked like if we ever did any actual work though, so it wasn't a complete loss.

There's another problem with the way we defer to data, and that is how it can blind us to the real world. A terrible and tragic example of this can be found with the Vietnam war.

I should say off the bat that I don't know anything about this war, and I'm just shamelessly lifting this view from a documentary I watched. The point really struck a chord with me though, so here it is.

Before Vietnam, wars had typically been fairly simple to track. There was a front line, and you tried to push the enemy back from it. If you pushed them back - you were winning. If they pushed you back - you were losing. Simple. Vietnam didn't have a front line though, so they couldn't use that to determine who was winning. In fact, there was no obvious metric the decision makers could use to determine who was winning at all. And because they couldn't find anything to measure that mattered, they decided to make what they could measure matter. So they decided that success would be measured by the number of enemy dead. As there were loads of dead people, the data suggested everything was going really well, and decisions were made on that basis. But the reality was those dead bodies were very often not the enemy. The data didn't reflect what was happening in the real world at all.

Now, imagine for a moment that they hadn't had any data. What if when they realised they couldn't measure anything that actually mattered, they just didn't measure anything at all. That sounds insane today, I know. But think it through. If they didn't measure anything, and they chose not to bring a bunch of meaningless numbers into a briefing room for them to base their decisions on, what would those leaders have had to have done? They would have had no choice - with no data, they would have had to have actually gone to Vietnam themselves. They'd have had to speak to the people who were fighting. They would have had to see the real world. They couldn't have just looked at a spreadsheet that said they were winning, made a totally misinformed decision that got a bunch of people killed, then gone back to playing golf. And if they had done that, they probably would have learned very quickly that things weren't going well. But the data they had access to gave them a proxy to the real world that allowed them to make decisions without engaging with that real world. And the data was wrong.

Data gives us a way to move a decision up a hierarchy, but that usually comes at the expense of all the nuance that would be necessary to make that decision well. The data tells some of the story, not all the story. But if you don't have time to understand the whole story, you shouldn't be making the decision. If you're forcing the person with the complete picture to condense all their understanding into a set of data that strips all context away, and then you're making the decision yourself based on this incomplete world view, you're going to get it wrong a lot of the time no matter how smart you are.

As I moved higher up in big organisations I started to see this lazy deferral to data play out more and more. I would sit in board meetings and watch a decision get made based on a number in a report that couldn't possibly reflect reality in any meaningful way. Having spent years of my early career working in almost every different role at the bottom of the org chart, it was fascinating to see just how disconnected the top of it could become as a result of this exponential simplification of facts. Foolish idealist that I am, I would often press for us to look beyond the numbers and consider what they actually meant for the people doing the work, and I'd usually be glared at as though I'd just opened a box of wasps in the middle of the boardroom. Nobody wanted the decision to become more difficult. The numbers made the decision easy, and that's all they wanted. People would rather be handed an easy lie than work for a difficult truth.

As a result of the management hierarchy demanding data from one another, we often focus more on reporting than we do on genuinely having an impact or understanding our actual reality. We all go around collecting data, and we come to think of that data as actually being the real world. We get lost in our spreadsheets, and we end up ignoring the things those spreadsheets are supposed to represent. I recently worked with a client who had asked for my help trying to get people more engaged at work. They had just performed an employee engagement survey, despite the fact they only had about 50 employees and every one of them worked in the same open plan office. If I had stood up and spoken loudly, every single employee could have heard me. I didn't even look at the results of the survey - I didn't need to - the fact they'd done it at all showed me what the root cause of the problem was. If you need to carry out a survey to find out the views of the 50 people in the same room as you, you're the one who isn't engaged. They were so obsessed with collecting data that they didn't do the one thing that would have actually engaged people - talk to them.

Far from giving us a view of the real world, I think data often obscures our view of it, and gives us an excuse not to put in the effort needed to truly understand it. We elevate its importance to an absurd level, and start to ignore the judgement of our staff and our colleagues as a result. Often we restrict people to only making decisions that they can validate with data - I once even saw a company that had written, "In God we trust - all others must bring data" in giant letters on their wall. In other words, "You're all idiots - we do not trust you". Wanting evidence that something is a good idea is of course not inherently wrong, but it's not always possible, and to actually believe that data always trumps human judgement is to completely dismiss the nature of creativity. The data often says the best ideas are wrong.

Before the iPhone was created, all the data said it was a stupid thing to create that nobody wanted. Steve Ballmer, then CEO of Microsoft, famously said, "There's no chance that the iPhone is going to get any significant market share. No chance." People love to beat him with that quote now, but if you make all your decisions and predictions based on data, you'd have said the same thing. If Steve Jobs had worked for you back then, you'd have told him to stop dicking about with that Jony Ive guy and bring you a tiny flip phone with buttons on it. According to all the data, making the iPhone was a stupid thing to do that was literally the opposite of what everyone wanted. Steve Ballmer wasn't the idiot, Steve Jobs was.

If all this sounds like heresy to you, don't worry. There's no need to round up the villagers just yet. None of this is to say I believe we shouldn't use data. I am not saying that at all. In fact, data is central to how I manage people. What I am saying is that the way hierarchical management depends on it can stifle the autonomy and growth our employees crave, and it can lead us to making bad decisions that make people feel ignored or unable to make an impact. Data is useful, but it isn't a replacement for human judgement and it shouldn't override it. It should help us make decisions, but we shouldn't be beholden to it. It's just data. It's not God.

Why It's Not Working - Recap

- **We haven't adapted to change** - The demands placed on managers have slowly become unrealistic, and technology has emerged that makes a lot of the tasks managers traditionally perform unnecessary

- **We solve problems with control and authority** - Managers are traditionally all chosen on the basis of having the same traits, and as a result the most common management solutions we tend to use stifle autonomy and growth

- **We cause new problems with our solutions** - By trying to control every aspect of what goes on with work we often create bad outcomes that wouldn't occur otherwise

- **We can't help everyone grow** - By taking on responsibility for how our staff grow and develop, we mismanage their expectations and damage our relationships

- **We have to worry about failure** - Because we're more concerned with avoiding failure than encouraging success, we implement processes and procedures that stifle our best performers

- **We have to measure everything** - We spend far too much time worrying about what we can measure and what we can prove, and often the data we gather does not truly reflect reality and leads to bad choices

3

MINIMUM EFFECTIVE MANAGEMENT

I want to reiterate that I haven't got any new management skills to share. There are some core skills that I think every manager needs (I have provided some guides to these skills in the *resources* section) but helping people improve these skills wasn't my intention when I started this process. I wanted to find a way to make being a manager easier, and to ensure that nobody that worked with me could ever be held back by their manager.

Yves Morieux says in his brilliant TED talk[2] that "the traditional pillars of management are obsolete". I agree with this completely. So rather than build around these obsolete pillars, I had to come up with some new ones.

---

[2] As work gets more complex, 6 rules to simplify, Yves Morieux, https://www.ted.com/talks/yves_morieux_as_work_gets_more_complex_6_rules_to_simplify

SOMETIMES WE'D EXPLODE AND DIE INSTEAD

Be like a pilot

A lot of the solutions traditional management gives us to our problems are fantastic in theory. When you look at what they're supposed to achieve for us, it makes perfect sense that we put so much effort into doing them. However, we tend to ignore their failure rate. These are often complex and difficult strategies to implement well, and when they aren't done well the consequences can be extremely disruptive. We often miss the fact that the management strategies we employ - however well intentioned - often don't go to plan, and when they don't go to plan they cause bigger problems than the ones they were intended to solve. We value them based on their intended outcomes, not the outcomes they actually generate.

Consider how commercial pilots fly planes. These pilots are not operating at the limit of their capabilities. They are all perfectly capable of performing far more complicated manoeuvres than they actually do. They could land in smaller spaces if required, operate in far more crowded airspace, fly faster, turn sharper. If we asked them to fly to the limits of their abilities, we'd often have much quicker flights. But sometimes, and not infrequently, we'd explode and die instead.

The reason we don't allow pilots to take greater risks isn't that we believe they aren't capable of *ever* flying to the standard necessary, or that we believe it wouldn't lead to faster flights on the occasions they did so successfully. We prevent them from flying this way because the chance of failure is too high, and they have people onboard that depend on them not to crash the plane. So, they fly at the optimal point between risk and performance, in such a way that will rarely result in failure but that still gets the job done. As a result, when a plane gets up in the air, we can be reasonably confident that it won't be on fire when it gets back down to the ground.

We currently do the opposite with managers. We give them a bunch of people to look after, then we push them to the absolute maximum of their management capabilities. Most of the time we don't even bother to train them first. So they crash. They crash all the time.

The first Minimum Effective Management pillar I decided on was that it would have to have a low accident rate. It would have to forgo complicated management activities that could easily go wrong, even if theoretically executing those activities perfectly might produce a great result. I wanted all my managers to be able to manage in a way that kept our accident rate pretty much on par with commercial pilots. It would still be a challenging role that would require skill to perform well, but we'd be doing it in such a way that we'd all get it right the overwhelming majority of the time.

As a result of this pillar, I had to ditch some activities that I'd had a lot of success with in the past. This wasn't because I believed those things never worked - I knew first-hand that they often did - it was because I knew they couldn't work consistently enough across my entire management team for us to depend on them.

AT LEAST ONE OF THOSE PEOPLE IS GOING TO BE A STUPID ASSHOLE

Build it for the best

A lot of managers - in fact I'm going to go as far as to say most managers - build the way they work around stifling the wrong behaviours, rather than around allowing the right ones to emerge. We look at the group of people you're part of and we think to ourselves, "At least one of those people is going to be a stupid asshole", then we treat you like a stupid asshole, just in case it's you.

We build our approaches to most situations around our worst people, not our best people. Imagine you have a group of people on one side of a ravine, and you need to get them all to the other side. You have a bunch of equipment, and you're in charge. So you spend hours planning exactly how they'll all get across. You make sure they're all in full safety gear, you tie them to each other with ropes, you explain to them exactly how they should cross, and you make sure everyone goes really slowly just in case they fall. Eventually, you get everyone to the other side, but it takes you forever. You managed them as if none of them were capable of getting to the other side safely without you, just because you knew at least one of them probably wasn't. This is the traditional management approach, and it's extremely frustrating for the people who are actually capable.

The comedian Jim Jefferies has a bit on this way of thinking. He talks about how the laws we set as a society must be based on the worst people in that society. We have to build around the stupid and irresponsible 1% who ruin it for the rest of us. We have to walk as slow as our slowest person. Whether it's taking drugs, driving a car, or owning a gun, our laws have to be set based on the most irresponsible people. When setting the laws for a society where the consequence of irresponsibility can easily mean people dying, this makes a lot of sense. But the same thinking need not apply to work where the consequences are almost certainly not going to be anything like as serious. We don't have to set our rules for the idiotic 1%, because our rules aren't going to mean the difference between life and death. We can do the opposite. We can assume that everyone is responsible, not that everyone is irresponsible.

So, instead of setting controlling rules that would stop people from making potentially damaging choices, I decided Minimum Effective Management would rely on safety nets that would provide protection when they did make them. If I had to get people to the other side of that ravine, I would do it differently. I would put up a safety net that would catch people if they fell, then I'd tell everyone to use their own judgement to get to the other side. Some people would do it easily, some people would ask for help, some people would struggle over on their own.

And some people would fall.

But I would have a safety net. The safety net would catch the people who didn't make it over, and those are the people I would then help get across. And because I wouldn't have wasted so much time controlling people who didn't need my help, I'd be able to give my full attention to the people who did actually need it. The end result would be that everyone would get to the other side much faster, with much less frustration, and I would have done much less work.

This was my next pillar. Instead of presuming people weren't responsible or capable, then controlling everyone to ensure nobody ever made mistakes, I would assume people were capable. But I'd protect them and myself from any consequences of them making mistakes. I would assume everyone could make the right decisions on how to get things done, without me supervising or guiding them. But I would put safety nets in place so I could identify the people who either couldn't or who didn't behave the way I needed them to. Then I'd focus all my management energy on the people that fell into the nets.

AUTOMATE, DECENTRALISE, OR STOP DOING IT ENTIRELY

Keep checking the pot

My next focus would be on technology. I would ditch the boiling frog mentality, and no longer do things a certain way just because that's the way they'd always been done. If the world had changed and given me a better way to do something, or made it so I didn't even need to do it anymore, I would adapt. I would reconsider every single management activity one by one - even those I believed in - and attempt to automate, decentralise, or stop doing them entirely.

When you really think about it, a lot of the management role is actually just moving information around. Today, technology can do a far better job of that than a human can. In a lot of cases, our involvement in moving this information around makes it less efficient, not more. I noticed that although we've all adopted a lot of new technology, we have often just overlaid it across our old way of doing things. It hasn't replaced things and made our jobs easier, it's added things and made our jobs harder. Every client I visit now uses Teams or Slack, and has set up a bunch of different channels dedicated to every topic imaginable - but they're still having just as many meetings as ever before, if not more. The tools provide us with virtual meetings room that anyone in the world can walk into at any time, so they should have enabled us to ditch those meetings. But instead, they've just given us an extra thing to manage.

To avoid these situations, I would rip everything out of the role, and only put back the things that technology couldn't do instead. There are so many great collaboration tools available now that almost any way of working can be supported off the shelf with a SaaS product that can be setup in minutes. So if I felt like technology could do something better than I could, then I'd let technology take care of it.

IF THIS SEEMS SCARY TO YOU, DON'T WORRY

Real autonomy

The next pillar was a tough one for me to accept. I would drop my treasured *they take the fame, you take the blame* mantra. I'd accept that in order to have real autonomy, not only would people have to be free to make their own decisions, they'd also have to be responsible for the consequences of them - good or bad.

In practise, the actual change I needed to make in my behaviour was tiny, but the change in outcome was huge.

Wait. I literally just thought of this. You could say it was…

One small step for a manager, one giant leap for management

I'm so sorry. I should be ashamed of myself. Never mind, I can edit that out later.

Ahem. Where was I? Right. The only change I needed to make - and I do mean the only one - was to change who had to convince who. With traditional management, a manager can just tell an employee what to do. If the employee wants to do something else, they'd need to convince the manager to let them. I was going to invert that. With Minimum Effective Management, if the manager wanted an employee to do something, they'd have to convince them. The final decision would always be made by the employee, not the manager.

This wouldn't mean the managers wouldn't be involved in decision making. In fact, nothing really had to change. As their managers, all the conversations we were having with our staff could still happen if we wanted them to. We could still be kept informed and completely up to date. We could be as connected to or disconnected from their work as we wanted to be. But our employees would understand that the decisions they made about how they worked and what they worked on would be theirs alone. If we wanted them to do something a certain way, but we couldn't convince them we were right, they could do what they wanted to do. The onus would be on us to convince them, not the other way around.

If this seems scary to you, don't worry. As I'll explain later on, there are safety nets. However, when I adopted this I was surprised at how unnecessary those safety nets turned out to be.

The first thing I noticed when I made this change was that my most belligerent employees - the ones who had previously seemed to challenge every decision I ever made - didn't behave anything like the way I had worried they might. I had worried they'd go rogue and do a bunch of potentially disruptive things, because when the decisions were mine they often pushed me to let them do precisely that. It stood to reason that without me to stop them, they'd charge off and cause a bunch of problems with their recklessness. That didn't happen. In fact, the moment those people were told that the choices were theirs - and along with the choices, the responsibility - they were suddenly much more open minded and keen to hear my point of view. What I realised is actually obvious in hindsight; when it's your choice and the consequences are on you, it's not so easy to be sure of yourself. It was much easier for them to complain about my decisions than it was for them to make those decisions themselves. Before, the consequence of failure was all mine, so they didn't really have to consider the risk, or worry about the fallout. They could complain at me for not making a specific decision without ever taking the time to think it through themselves, because they knew that if I eventually cracked and agreed with them, it would still be my fault if things went wrong. The decision actually being theirs changed that dynamic entirely. And they responded to that.

Not only that, I was a little upset to learn that it turns out I'm not right as often as I thought I was. I am naturally a stubborn guy, so I used to pretty much always get my own way. That's not to say that I would never listen to people or that I was unreceptive to having my mind changed. I was always open to being convinced, and I would frequently have my mind changed by a well-made argument, but I would actually have to have my mind changed. If you couldn't change my mind, we were going to do things my way. And because I was stubborn, once I did get my own way things very rarely went wrong, because I would work damn hard to make sure they didn't. This made me feel as though I very rarely made mistakes, which in turn probably made me even more stubborn. But the thing with getting your own way all the time is that you never get to see what would have happened if you hadn't got your own way. There's no control group. So when I started to let people do things that I didn't agree with, I noticed that things I thought were going to go wrong in fact often went very well. A lot of the time great things would happen that would never have happened if we'd done things my way. And because people were working on something they truly believed in and had fought to do, they were totally invested in making it successful. All of a sudden, instead of my stubbornness being the tool I relied on to be successful, it was the stubbornness of others. They were the ones who had decided to do what they were doing, so they were absolutely determined to prove themselves right.

The opposite was true when I'd been making all the decisions. When every decision was mine, even when people agreed with those decisions, they didn't have that same depth of personal drive for things to go well. With this new way of working, even when people made the same choice I would have made anyway, they were far more invested in making it a success. What I found was that when the choices were theirs, and the responsibility was theirs, that's when they were their most engaged.

So the next pillar of Minimum Effective Management would be that people could choose what they worked on and how they approached it. If they never had to do anything they didn't decide to do themselves, then the consequences of their actions could only ever be their responsibility. And as I mentioned earlier, I don't believe I have to do anything to give this responsibility to people. Responsibility for your own actions is inalienable. We should never have taken it away, but traditional management did precisely that. With Minimum Effective Management I just stop doing that. I don't swallow that fly.

Note: There is an important caveat to this. There are of course times when I really can't be flexible. When I know that no matter what, I need to make the decision on what we do. In those situations, I don't mess people about. I don't pretend that it's still their decision if it isn't. I'm just honest. If they've walked into a room with me and the dynamic has changed - I'm up front about it. I just say "I need the decision on what we do with this to be mine" and they always understand and accept it. I still have all the same conversations I would have had anyway, I've just taken responsibility for the decision myself.

ACHIEVE EVERYTHING

BY DOING NOTHING

Group recognition

My approach to traditional management always heavily relied on understanding how different people respond to incentives. There are always a range of incentives at play in any given situation, and understanding those was always key to me being able to shape how my teams behaved. In the simplest terms, we all respond to three different kinds of incentives:

- Social - How we're perceived by others

- Economic - How we personally benefit

- Moral - What we believe is right or wrong

There are positive and negative versions of each of these, and whether we experience the result of them immediately or in the future has an impact as well. So there are effectively twelve different kinds of incentive a manager can leverage to get people to behave the way we want them to; social, economic and moral, each with a positive and a negative variation, and each of those with a future and a present variation.

But people all respond to them differently. Some people

don't care about moral incentives at all - they will quite happily do something they believe is morally wrong if it means they will economically benefit. Some people are the opposite, and will do what they think is right even if it comes at great personal cost. Some people are willing to suffer today in order to benefit in the future. Others will do things they want to do today despite knowing it will cause problems for them later on. Some people are more motivated to avoid a bad thing than try for a good thing. When you take out insurance for example, you're worried about a bad thing happening. When you bet on a horse though, you're hoping for a good thing to happen. Either way, you're betting on an outcome, you're just being driven to do it by a different variation of an economic incentive. When you take out home insurance, you're actually just betting against your insurance company that your house will burn down. You bet it will, they bet it won't. You're betting on the bad thing happening. When you bet on a horse, you're betting on the good thing happening. I know many people who find the idea of not having insurance terrifying, but who would never bet on a horse with the same odds of winning as their house has of burning down. I also know many people who think insurance is stupid, but who play the lottery every week. What it comes down to is this - all of us respond slightly differently to each different kind of incentive.

But the vast majority of us respond extremely strongly to social incentives. Humans are social animals and our ability to co-operate and function in social groups is how we survived as a species. Generally speaking, what people think about us matters to each of us a great deal. Even to the people who say they don't care about it. After all, if they don't care what people think, why would it be important to them that people knew that? I suspect that the rise of social media has made this response even stronger. I think what people think of us is probably more important than ever. In almost all situations, we can be very confident that social incentives are going to be by far the most effective way to shape behaviours, but traditional management often gets in the way of us using them at work.

Several years ago I took over a team that had been struggling for some time. During the handover, the outgoing manager ran me through what had been going on. It was a customer service team that was very data centric, and it was possible to see exactly how much work each individual had been doing. Initially, the problem the team had was that most staff had consistently been having days where they just didn't deal with many requests. There were a few people who had been excelling and largely carrying the rest of the team, but not enough to mean that the overall performance was acceptable. That was the initial problem, and in a bid to improve things the manager had set people individual targets for the number of requests they had to deal with. After he did that, things got worse. Although the worst offenders improved once they had specific targets to hit, the performance of the people who had been excelling and carrying the rest of the team dropped. Overall, results become worse than they had been before. The manager had spent huge amounts of time in meetings and performance management sessions. He'd taken disciplinary action. He'd tried the carrot and the stick. Nothing had improved. The result was always an underperforming, unmotivated and unhappy team.

The problem was the incentives.

Before I go on, I should clarify what I mean by an economic incentive. It's easy to assume that they just relate to money, but they can actually be anything that relates to you directly benefiting or suffering. An economic incentive can simply mean you having an experience you like or don't like. If your manager asks you to do something, and the reason you decide to do it is simply that you don't want to get shouted at, this is you responding to a negative economic incentive. You're avoiding a bad experience. If you come into work and you want to disappear into a YouTube hole rather than doing work you find boring, that's a positive economic incentive. You want a good experience.

In this case, when the manager had given people individual targets, he had created two new economic incentives, one negative and one positive. But he'd also messed with the moral incentives. The negative economic incentive was simply that he would privately call people out if they didn't hit their targets, which is obviously an experience most people would want to avoid. The positive economic incentive related to their bonus. He connected their targets to their bonus payments, so the more consistently they hit their targets, the higher their bonus would be. As I'll explain in a moment, those incentives didn't result in anyone's behaviour improving, but before I get to that, let's talk about why the performance actually got worse.

Previously, the team had been carried by the exceptional performers. They had been delivering far more work than the minimum requirement the manager stated in the targets he set. But once he set those targets, he had effectively told those exceptional performers that if they hit that target, it was perfectly acceptable for them to just stop working. Previously, they had just been doing as much as they could do, because that seemed like the right thing to do. He changed that. He told them it was acceptable for them to do less. So they did.

This might have been a price worth paying if the other incentives he'd put in place at the same time had resulted in the rest of the team getting significantly better. That didn't happen though. Let's break down both those incentives and take a look at why they made very little difference.

Firstly, the negative one: getting called out for not hitting your targets. He wasn't the shouting type, he was a supportive and generally nice guy. If someone had consistently missed their targets he would have taken action, but it would never have been anything aggressive. It's not like he would have yelled or screamed at anyone. The conversation wouldn't have been unpleasant at all. So when someone came into work tired, or hungover, or just feeling lazy, the positive economic incentive of just taking it easy and looking at Instagram all day was usually a lot stronger than the negative incentive of avoiding a slightly awkward conversation with their manager a few days later.

It's not hard to imagine why that negative incentive didn't really change much for people who hadn't previously been working hard. If they didn't care before, that incentive was unlikely to change anything.

But what about if we factor in the positive economic incentive. After all, their bonus was riding on them hitting their targets. That should have made a difference, surely?

Actually, not one bit. Each person's bonus payment was determined based on them hitting their targets each month. The bonus was paid annually, and each person could receive up to a maximum of 10% of their salary. However - and I'm sure this will resonate with you if you have a bonus scheme - in practise, the variable range of that bonus wasn't really between 0-10%. Realistically, it was between 6-9%. Nobody ever really got less than 6%. It just didn't happen. Someone would have had to have done practically no work at all to be given under 6%. At the same time, the standard required to be given 10% was so laughably high that very few people got that either. Most people knew they were out of the running for 10% by the end of the first month of the year, so really, the amount any one person's bonus could vary depending on their performance was only about 4% over the entire year. And that's only 0.33% per month. That's a near homeopathic level of dilution. Would that make you do something you didn't want to do on any given day?

When you consider all the incentives in play - the ones created by the manager and the ones that were just inherent - you realise that it isn't surprising at all that their behaviours didn't improve. He had given them targets on paper, but as I'll explain in more detail later on, he hadn't finished the job. He hadn't made them actually want to hit them, not really. The incentives weren't there. The prospect of possibly securing an extra 0.33% of their salary to be paid to them several months later wasn't as enticing as the prospect of looking at videos of dogs all day. The reluctance to have a slightly awkward conversation in a couple of weeks was not as strong as the reluctance to deal with a bunch of horrible tasks they didn't want to do right at that very moment.

When all was said and done, after everything he did - after painstakingly setting and tracking the goals, after planning the bonus structure, after diligently having the meetings and carrying out the performance management, after all that - the incentives he'd put in play achieved almost nothing.

And he could have achieved everything he needed to achieve with social incentives, if he'd actually done almost nothing himself.

When I took over the team, I removed all the goals and targets. I told everyone that the expectation of them was to handle all the requests the team received to the highest standard possible. I set no targets, either individually or for the group. I defined no minimum requirements. I just told them to do their best. Then I made all the data that showed how the team was performing - and how each individual was contributing to that performance - available to everyone. Live. Not filtered through a manager, not shared through a presentation or privately in one-on-one meetings. All of it was available live to anyone who wanted to see it. In fact, I displayed that performance data on a screen in the middle of the office. Everyone could see what was actually happening and who was doing what.

An important thing to reiterate here is that that's all I did. I set no expectations regarding the amount of work an individual was required to do. There were no consequences or rewards. If someone wanted to do absolutely no work, that was entirely up to them. But if they chose to do that, their coworkers would see it. They wouldn't be able to hide behind their manager. I said to them, "You are responsible for what this team achieves", then I provided them the means to see what the team was achieving and who was doing what to make that happen.

Within days, all the problems went away. Everyone was working hard, and the request queue was gone. Everyone on the team was happier and more engaged with their work. And not a single management activity had been carried out. Nobody had been told what to do, controlled, or disciplined. There was no conflict, people just took responsibility, did the work they needed to do, and helped each other when they needed it. I hadn't had a single conversation with anyone about their work.

This change happened because by getting out of the way, I'd put the social incentives back in play. I'd enabled one of the core things people have been telling us they want - recognition. As managers when we hear that our staff want more recognition, egomaniacs that we are, we tend to think that means from us. We then make sure we praise them more, or thank them regularly. But that isn't it. That's reductive. That's not what true recognition is, and it's not the recognition people really want. Unfortunately, even though we're their manager, we're generally not so revered that a simple attaboy from us will give people a sense of validation and self-worth. You might be that person to them - and if you are good for you - but most of us aren't (definitely not one in seven of us) and most of us are not so important to our staff that our opinion of them will significantly shape how they feel about themselves. But if their peers all think they're brilliant, and their peers all look up to them and appreciate them, that's usually a different story.

There's also another aspect to recognition that often gets overlooked, and that's that it goes both ways. To keep us motivated, we don't just need people to notice when we do well. We need people to notice when we do badly too. Much in the same way that some people would always buy insurance but never bet on a horse, some people aren't too concerned with their peers thinking they're brilliant, but they wouldn't want to be thought of as being lazy or letting the group down. They would work hard to avoid that. Some people are more motivated by the negative social incentive than the positive one.

Rightly or wrongly, we also measure ourselves against other people. We don't just want people to know and acknowledge when we are doing well, we want to relate that recognition to the recognition received by the people around us. Throughout my career, I've coached countless people who told me they were frustrated because a colleague wasn't pulling their weight, and their manager wasn't calling them out on it. These people were very rarely suffering any direct consequences of their colleague not working hard - they just didn't feel it was fair. They didn't want more recognition themselves, they just didn't want the same amount of recognition as someone who didn't deserve it. Often when people believe that their coworkers aren't working as hard as they are, but are still getting the same amount of recognition, this leads to them becoming demotivated and working less. They don't see the point in working hard if it doesn't make any difference anyway. It can become a race to the bottom. But when the fact they're working harder or contributing more to the group is being recognised, this is no longer the case.

This all forms the basis for my next pillar - group recognition. I wouldn't think of myself as an idolised parent who could single-handedly provide a sense of validation to all of my staff. I would create a workplace where recognition wouldn't be something the managers would need to give people, but would instead be something they could get from one another. With Minimum Effective Management, how an individual was contributing wouldn't be something secret that only the manager knew, and it wouldn't be something that only the manager measured. The value of our contribution to the group would be evaluated and communicated by the group itself.

WHAT THE HELL IS GOING ON?!

Open information

The next pillar leads on from the previous ones. If everyone would be making their own choices, I would need to make sure they had access to all the information they needed in order to do so as well as possible.

Controlling information is one of those management activities that takes up a bunch of our time and almost certainly does more harm than good in the long run. There's a common behavioural trap that many leaders fall into. I've certainly been the victim of it, and I've certainly done it myself in the past. The behaviour is what I call the *what would have to be true* trick. To be honest that's pretty much just a complicated term for lying, but I think calling it a lie implies a more sinister intention than the one that drives managers when we employ this trick. When we use this trick, we actually have good intentions. We're trying to get the best outcomes for everyone, but we're doing it by either withholding information, or by being outright dishonest.

This is how it plays out. We have decided that the best outcome for everyone would be achieved if people behaved a certain way. Unfortunately, we also believe that if they had all the information about the current situation, they wouldn't behave in that way. We think that if they knew what was actually true, a lot of them might behave in a way that would create a bad outcome for everyone, including themselves. So, to enable the good outcome for everyone, we decide to tell them something else is true. We create what we think the necessary reality would be in order to get people to behave the way we need them to, then we tell them that's the way things actually are.

One of the most common ways I've seen this being done is when the company is in financial trouble, and management hides this from the employees. They worry that if the employees know the company isn't secure, they'll quit to find one that is, and that this would exacerbate the problems and make a bad outcome more likely. So management pretends that everything is fine. I've been on the wrong end of this a couple of times. I once had a job where two thirds of the staff were laid off, and almost none of us had had any clue the company had been in a position where that was even a possibility. As far as we were aware, we'd been thriving. And to be honest, as a result of believing that, a lot of people had lacked any urgency with the way they worked. A lot of them had spent more time playing foosball than they had spent working. Management had been telling them everything was going great, so they didn't see the need to work any harder than they already were. If everyone had known the urgency of the situation, I don't doubt that some people would have panicked and quit for a more secure job. But a lot of people loved that company and they would have wanted to help save it. Those people would have rallied around and done everything in their power to fix the problems if they'd known about them. Instead, they all just lost their jobs one day.

Controlling the narrative was one of the things I found most frustrating about managing within a complex organisation. Whenever I was in a meeting and I heard someone say words to the effect of "how do we communicate this to people", I would immediately find myself irritated. There always seemed to be two jobs to do – working out what was actually true, then working out what we were going to tell people was true. This seemed to be the case in every direction: up, down or across the org chart, everyone seemed to be constructing their ideal version of reality to tell one another. It was maddening, and a total waste of time. Everything is so much easier when everyone is just honest, even if the consequences of being honest might be bad sometimes.

The primary reason for this pillar isn't that constructing narratives is time consuming though. It's that it creates a barrier. I strongly believe that we have to think of work relationships exactly as we think of any other human relationship. When we get to work we don't suddenly become a different creature. We're all still humans. This means that the same rules should apply to how we build relationships, and every successful relationship is built on trust and honesty. We tend to have an expectation of our staff to bring all their beneficial human traits into work, but leave their troublesome ones at home. I don't believe that's possible. We come as a package. If you want my good traits, you get all my traits. If you want my passion and my drive and my enthusiasm, you can't lie to me and expect me not to get pissed off, or to stop trusting you. I can't act like a professional robot and dismiss a natural human reaction just because it's what has been determined to be professional behaviour. You don't buy my trust just be virtue of employing me. You have to earn it.

When we try to control and manipulate information to make people behave the way we want them to, even with good intentions, we often lose all control instead. If we tell a lie to get what we want, some people are going to see through the lie, but still not know the truth. They will then create their own truth, and they'll likely make us the villain because they'll know we're lying to them but they won't know why. When we don't tell people what is actually happening, we don't bring them into the problems and we don't allow them to help us solve them. I don't pretend we're not risking a bad outcome by being totally open, but by being withholding we're pretty much guaranteeing there won't be a good outcome. It's such an unambitious and time consuming way to operate.

This is the final pillar of Minimum Effective Management. If I know something, my staff will know it too. No varnishing, no protecting, no coddling. We will all have the same information. We'll all be in it together.

The Minimum Effective Management pillars

- **Keep management activities simple** - We should only use management activities that will nearly always work as intended. Reliable is better than perfect

- **Assume people will do a good job** - Our assumption should be that everyone is capable and will behave the right way. We won't implement policies that prevent mistakes at the expense of autonomy

- **Automate and decentralise** - No management activity should ever be carried out simply because it's the way it has always been done previously. Technology can solve many of the problems traditionally solved by managers

- **Give people real autonomy** - People should decide for themselves what they work on and how they will approach that work

- **Group recognition** - There should be no performance review run by a manager. People should provide ongoing feedback to one another based on the work they're involved with

- **Open information** – There should be no controlled narratives. Everyone should know everything that is going on in the place they work so that they're able to help solve the problems

These are the non-negotiables of any technique or practise I rely on to achieve the things I'm supposed to achieve as a manager. If there's a management practice that goes against any of these principles, I don't do it, even if I've had good results with it before.

By sticking to these principles, I've been able to create the kind of workplaces that I would want to work and manage in. Our managers are no longer high pressure points of failure who are responsible for the actions of other people. Instead they're equal members of a team that are all working together to achieve common goals. Our approach allows people to thrive, but it doesn't coddle or baby them. We give them the things they want, and we expect them to prove us right to do that. They're given all the opportunities to succeed that we can possibly give them, but they have to seek out and take those opportunities. They aren't handed to them on a plate. Everyone knows the expression "you can lead a horse to water, but you can't make it drink". Well I think of this approach as one step back from that. We don't even lead the horses to water - we just make sure there is water, and we trust the horses to find it.

4

GETTING WHAT I NEED

As I mentioned in the introduction, I wanted to avoid making this book an instruction manual. One of the reasons for this is that there really aren't any specific activities that I consider an essential part of Minimum Effective Management. The principles are what matter. Any activity that fits with those core principles is perfectly valid. I don't consider this to be a management framework in the purest sense. There's no rigidity to how the approach calls for different people or situations to be managed.

That being said, I've obviously had to develop specific ways to meet the needs of my role that do fit with these new principles. What I've tried to do here is explain what those things are and why I do them, but that doesn't mean I consider them to be the only way to achieve things.

Perhaps what is more important than explaining what I do, is explaining what I don't do. The approach is called Minimum Effective Management after all, so it stands to reason that I've taken more away than I've added. When I've stopped doing something that's a core part of traditional management, I make sure to take the time to explain in detail why I've stopped doing it, and why I'm getting the results I need anyway.

There is a structure to the way I present this, but it is a loose one. I tried to walk through everything in a methodical way, moving through from goal setting to delegating, executing and measuring. However, the nature of the approach means that a lot of the activities I've added or removed touch all of those aspects at once. I'm reluctant to use the word, but it's kind of holistic. Most of the things managers do tend to have a far-reaching impact, so it's not easy to compartmentalise them. I might have stopped doing something that was perfectly delivering the thing it was supposed to deliver, but that was also causing problems further down the road with something else. I consider how any action taken may affect every part of the job, so the focus of a given explanation can jump around from time to time.

Regardless of the structure of how it's presented, I hope that I've adequately explained how I meet all the requirements asked of a modern manager, without working anywhere near as hard.

I DON'T CARE IF YOU CAN MEASURE THE PAST

I CARE IF YOU CAN SHAPE THE FUTURE

Communicating goals

Before I get going with this, I should be clear on the reason I set goals in the first place. Traditionally goals are used not just to communicate what the company is trying to accomplish, but also to communicate what departments or individuals should try to accomplish, and sometimes as a basis for evaluating the performance of those departments and individuals.

I don't do this. I think that whenever we try to use one tool to achieve several different things, we tend to dilute its effectiveness for its primary function. When it comes to setting goals, the most valuable thing this activity can give us is a common purpose which everyone understands. But when we give people individual goals we tend to gear those goals towards guiding and measuring them personally, and this usually comes at the expense of obscuring the company purpose. We end up not achieving the most important thing goals need to achieve. Therefore I ignore all the reasons to set goals other than ensuring people understand what the company itself is trying to accomplish. The other things goals are often used for are achieved elsewhere.

One other thing before I start, for the goals I do set, I don't use anything ground-breaking. Objectives and Key Results (OKRs) are a great way to structure goals and I haven't felt the need to reinvent that particular wheel. If you're unfamiliar with OKRs, it's not a problem. You can set your goals however you choose, I just happen to prefer OKRs (there's a brief guide to them in the *resources* section at the end of the book).

The power of goals

It is near universally accepted that people who have clearly defined goals are more likely to achieve good results than people who don't. There's an urban legend about a study conducted at Harvard Business School relating to this. The actual legend is more detailed than I have presented here, but the gist of it is that a group of Harvard students were asked if they had set themselves written goals for their career. Only 3% of them said they had. The study then checked back on everyone several years later, and found that the 3% who had given themselves written goals had made more money than the other 97% combined. When I first heard this I thought it was a true story, but I've since learned that it almost certainly didn't actually happen. Regardless of that, it felt plausible enough to me at the time that I believed it. It still seems plausible to me today in fact - but only because that 3% would have set their goals themselves.

An idea has prevailed that we can just give people goals, and that action in and of itself will achieve something. I've never seen any evidence that this is correct. A couple of years ago I was working with an exec team to help them with a productivity problem. I asked the group how they were approaching goal setting. One guy - who had been particularly defensive about my involvement - confidently declared that everyone on his team had clear goals. He stated it as though that should be the end of the matter; that there was no way a lack of clarity on the goals could have been part of the problem and I should just move on. I wasn't convinced. So I asked him if he'd mind if I spoke to someone on his team, and he agreed, quite certain that what he'd told me was true.

So I left the meeting room and went out into the office to speak to someone from his team, with the execs unsubtly watching on through the glass meeting room wall. Our conversation went something like this:

"Have you got goals you're trying to achieve at the moment?"

"Oh sure, I've been given goals"

"Great, what are they?"

"Just a second, I'll just get the file up"

He then opened up a document that had his goals written in it, and he read them to me. They were very clear and very sensible. They were very well set goals. I couldn't fault them one bit.

I then went back to the meeting room and told everyone that he didn't have any goals.

His manager was furious. "I just saw him show them to you!" he raged. I then explained something to him that managers consistently fail to understand. A goal - a genuine goal - is something you want to achieve. It's the *wanting* it that makes it more likely to happen. But if you need to check a file to find out what that thing even is, then you obviously don't really want it. That goal isn't truly your goal, and it's unlikely to make the slightest difference to your behaviour.

A few years ago I wanted a dog. If someone had asked me, "Hey Matt, do you want a dog?", I wouldn't have said, "Hold on a moment, let me check the file". I'd have immediately said, "Yes".

I have a dog now.

Giving someone a list of things we want them to achieve doesn't give them goals. It allows us to tick off the *give people goals* item from our to do list, but it doesn't really achieve the thing that would actually help us get the results we want.

Actually giving someone a goal is far more complex. We need them to believe in it, we need them to want it, we need them to be incentivised to achieve it - either morally, economically or socially. It is not as simple as taking them into a room and saying "here are your goals". The fact we reduce it to that level is why we fail at it so often, but we reduce it to that level because doing it any other way is far too time consuming and difficult to do at any kind of scale. If we actually did it properly, we would barely have time to do anything else. So we do it in a way that doesn't usually work, just so we can say we've done it. Then we're surprised when it doesn't achieve what we want it to.

Even on the occasions we do successfully assign a goal to someone in such a way that it becomes something they genuinely want to achieve, this often creates conflicting incentives and encourages game playing. Not too long ago I spoke to a marketer who had been set the goal of gaining a certain number of social media followers for his company. His bonus was connected to the success of this goal. So he simply paid a few dollars and bought the followers he needed so he could achieve it. He'd been given no incentive for those followers to bring any value to the business. You might think he acted immorally - and obviously he did - but for this individual the economic incentive obviously outweighed the moral one, and besides, the goals he had been given were supposed to give him total clarity on what he was supposed to achieve. And he achieved his goals. If he was required to use his judgement to interpret his individual goals the correct way, then they really didn't deliver any more value than just asking him to interpret the company goals would have delivered. In fact, as it turned out, they delivered considerably less value.

Setting individual or team goals takes time, it adds complexity, and it creates conflicting incentives. There is also often a trade-off between connecting people to the true company purpose, and giving people a goal they feel they can directly control. Not too long ago I was speaking to a friend who was annoyed because she had been set a revenue based goal by her manager, despite the fact her role wasn't directly revenue generating. She was quite justifiably frustrated by it, even though generating more revenue for the company is ultimately what everyone is really employed to do. When we set someone an individual goal, we're tacitly telling them that they - and they alone - are responsible for achieving it, so they get annoyed when we give them a goal that isn't entirely in their control. In today's working world though, there are very few things that are worth achieving that can be achieved by one person alone. Individual goals by their very nature work against collaboration, or shouldn't actually be individual goals in the first place.

I'm not saying it's impossible to set good individual goals. Of course it isn't. You might do it perfectly. But will you do it perfectly across all your people, every single time you do it?

Will all the managers in your company get it right every single time across all of their people? Of course not. No matter how talented a manager is, they are going to get this wrong sometimes. And when we set goals people can't influence, or don't believe in, or that don't incentivise them to behave in ways that will help achieve the primary company goals, we create a whole raft of new problems. On balance I'm certain that even the most talented managers get this wrong often enough that the problems caused far outweigh the benefit gained.

Not only that, but getting them right doesn't even matter most of the time. You can deliver a perfect set of goals that complement each other and turn your team into a highly motivated and well-oiled machine, but it probably won't matter because the world doesn't care one bit about your plans. The situation you created your goal setting masterpiece for will very likely change almost immediately.

This used to happen to me all the time. I would spend days crafting goals for all of my staff. I would create a perfectly balanced dance of incentives, ensuring each person would behave in just the right way to generate the outcomes I needed. I'd painstakingly ensure that everyone had been given goals that made their exact responsibilities perfectly clear, that they were fully in control of achieving, and that would ensure my own goals would be achieved. I remember countless late nights tweaking and fiddling, making sure everything was just right.

Then in a matter of days, something would change that none of us had predicted, and the whole house of cards would fall down.

The problem with giving people total clarity of purpose is

that you also create rigidity, and you put people in silos. When people are given their own goals, those goals become more important to them than the other goals the business has, regardless of their true value to the business as a whole. We are very rarely set goals that fully cover the contribution we are going to need to make, and the majority of the time we will help out with things unrelated to our goals anyway. This just goes to show that we don't need to be given individual goals to begin with. We can use our judgement to determine the best way to be helpful, if we just know what the company is trying to achieve.

When we set people specific goals, we complicate any restructuring of our plans that may be needed in order to adapt to a new situation. If we need to give people a new focus, we have to adjust their goals, and work out some kind of plan for how we will evaluate them given that their goals changed midway through the review period. The goal setting we carry out to help provide clarity often just becomes an administrative hindrance.

Across most of my career, any individual goals I have been set usually only stayed relevant for a few weeks at the most. The vast majority of times - because my managers couldn't see into the future - our situation changed in ways none of us completely predicted and my goals became less relevant. The solution to this that most of my managers opted for was to just decide to ignore the goals that had become irrelevant. This was the best option - just ignoring the activity entirely. However, I can remember several instances where managers couldn't bring themselves to ignore the process, and marked me down on a review because I hadn't achieved a goal that they themselves had prevented me working on.

Things had changed and higher value work had emerged, so I'd been tasked to do that work instead. The company was better off as a result of me doing it - but I was then punished. If I'd done what I had been incentivised to do and focused on my own goals, everyone other than me would have been worse off. In these situations success was achieved in spite of the way I was managed, not because of it. That is a completely unacceptable outcome for a management activity, but not an uncommon one.

Again, I don't claim it's impossible to get this right. I've managed to get all my goal setting right a few times over my career. But it's a lot of effort and there's huge scope for getting it wrong. You have to be a really good manager to consistently set individual or departmental goals that motivate people to behave in exactly the way you need them to without creating conflicting incentives, and you have to be really lucky and hope the world doesn't change around you even if you pull that off. Put simply, it's an activity with far too high a failure rate to fit with the principles of Minimum Effective Management.

To come up with an alternative way of working, I looked at how traditional management had come to so heavily rely on individual goal setting. I felt that understanding this would help me avoid repeating the same mistakes when deciding on a new approach.

What this immediately showed me was that individual goal setting is a boiling frog solution. When the requirement of sharing goals emerged, sharing all the information necessary to allow everyone to work on the same small set of company goals wasn't possible. It would have been a shambles if we'd tried. If everyone in a company had just worked on a single set of company goals without any division of focus, nobody would ever have known who was doing what, and people would constantly have been tripping over one another. Some work would have been done multiple times, other work wouldn't have been done at all. There would have been gaps and overlaps and confusion. Some goals would have received too much focus, some wouldn't have received enough. The likelihood of them all being achieved without exercising more control would have been incredibly low. So we used cascading or aligned goal structures that allowed us to divide the responsibility across the whole of the company. We essentially said, "Ok, in order for the company to achieve xyz, you guys need to achieve x, you guys need to achieve y, and you guys need to achieve z". It was a rigid approach, but in a world where every employee was unable to share information with everyone else instantly, it was a necessary one.

Today, the problem that led to that decision doesn't exist. We don't have the same restrictions when it comes to sharing information. We have technology that enables anyone to stay completely connected to what everyone else is doing anywhere in the world, with next to no effort at all. If we use the tools that are available, we can pretty much effortlessly see exactly what is going on with coworkers, who is doing what, and how well things are going. We can easily talk to whoever we need to talk to to get the information we need before making a decision on what we are going to do to contribute to a company goal. The necessity for a rigid cascaded or aligned goal structure is gone. We can be dynamic and agile instead, and all work together on the true company purpose.

Having a shared purpose

I decided that I wanted to work in a way that would connect everyone to the same core set of company goals. Nobody would have their own goal. Instead, we'd all have all the goals. If we all had a common purpose that was communicated through a common set of goals, there would never be any chance of confusion or conflicting incentives. It would also mean that the work necessary to truly connect people to those goals and give them a real desire to see them achieved could be done collectively, not at an individual level. If a sense of purpose is one of the core things a modern employee desires, what better way to provide this than ensuring the true purpose of the company is something shared by everyone.

This has also meant that my goal setting is incredibly simple. My leadership team and I decide what the company is trying to achieve, we set our goals accordingly, then we make sure everyone always knows what those goals are and how they're progressing. We then ask everyone to help us achieve them. All of them. The best way they know how. That's it. Everyone that works with us is trying to achieve all of our goals, and we never cascade, align, or dilute them.

To make this work, I have to ensure that people understand how they can best help us achieve those goals at any given time. To do this in a way that would fit with the Minimum Effective Management principles, I had to completely reimagine the way we connect people to company goals. With traditional management, the relationship we create between each employee and the company goals is based on division of responsibility - each person is given their own goal that contributes in some way to one of the top level company goals. This has been the uniform way people have traditionally been connected to goals. But I realised that in practice this makes little sense, as there are actually three different types of relationship that a person within any organisation might have with the company goals:

- **Decision Makers** - Decision makers are people who decide on specific work to be carried out in order to achieve the goals. They don't necessarily do that work. These might be your project managers, product owners, or departmental heads

- **Implementers** - Implementers are people who carry out specific tasks designed to help achieve the goals. They don't decide what the work is. These might be your software engineers, designers, etc

- **Maintainers** - Maintainers are people who perform regular recurring tasks in order to help achieve the goals, or support others around them. They don't work on specific project based tasks the way the Implementers do. These are the customer service agents, the salespeople, etc

These different relationships mean that people should be connected to the company goals in different ways. Everyone should still be responsible for achieving all of the goals, but depending on their role in the business, they should interact with them differently.

Decisions Makers and Implementers

I'll explain how I connect the Decision Makers and Implementers to the goals at the same time, as their roles are interconnected.

When it comes to project based work, I think of these two relationships in the context of a work menu:

- **Decision Makers** decide what goes on the menu

- **Implementers** make selections from the menu

What this means is that they contribute to the success or failure of the goals very differently. Decision Makers can contribute with their choices - by putting the right things on the menu. Implementers can contribute with their behaviours - by delivering the things that are put on the menu as effectively as possible. An Implementer's perfect execution of a bad idea won't see the goals being achieved, but a great idea implemented poorly won't see them achieved either. Their relationship to the goals is entirely different, so they need to have different responsibilities.

To enable us to all work towards the same set of company goals, the responsibilities we give people are:

- **Decision Makers** are expected to know what all the company goals are, what work is being done to achieve them, and how they're progressing

- **Implementers** are expected to know which goals the projects they are working on are supposed to help achieve

It may not be obvious at first glance, but by simply making sure the above two things are true, I get everything I need from goal setting. The people who decide what work will take place know what the company is trying to achieve and how well that's progressing, so they can make decisions on that basis with all the pertinent information. The people doing the work understand what that work is intended to help achieve and are able to frame their decisions and approaches on that basis, meaning the true purpose of what they're doing is never hidden and no conflicting incentives are ever accidentally created.

The execution of this is extremely simple. When Decision Makers create a new project, they align that project to the specific company goals they're trying to influence. Then, whenever an Implementer starts to work on that Project, they make sure they know what those connected goals are. This means that instead of Implementers being given their own individual goals, they just **inherit the goals from whatever they are working on** at any given time.

When it comes to the Implementers, this approach - whilst completely effortless for the managers - negates all the problems caused by individual goal setting, and achieves everything the activity is supposed to achieve but typically fails to. It gives people complete clarity of purpose, but doesn't create any rigidity. If someone switches to work on a different project temporarily, or permanently, nothing needs to change from an admin standpoint. Someone can move to a new project, inherit a new goal, and everything is still completely clear. A person can work on five projects and have five different goals, or work on one project and have one goal. There is nothing that can happen that will generate more admin for the manager, and there is zero opportunity for confusion.

For Decision Makers, the relationship with the goals is different. Decision Makers are responsible for deciding what work gets done - or what goes on the work menu - so the relationship I need to forge between them and the goals is different. Decision Makers need to know how all the goals are progressing, so they can make informed decisions on what we need to deliver.

As I mentioned earlier, the traditional solution to this has been division of responsibility. We would give one person one goal, and another person another. They would then each be responsible for achieving 'their' goal. Working this way, we ensured that each goal would get an equal amount of attention. But this is the safety rule approach. This is us making sure we avoid the undesired outcome of a goal not getting enough focus, by limiting an individual's ability to direct their focus towards any goal they believe needs it the most.

As I don't use safety rules, I put up a safety net instead. Rather than giving everyone a specific goal in order to make sure that goal gets enough focus, I instead make sure we can all see how much focus each of the goals may need at any given time.

This proved incredibly simple to do:

- All the Decision Makers are tasked with achieving all the company goals

- Each goal is given a representative (not an owner). This representative ensures all the relevant information regarding a goal is collected and shared with the group, but who is no more responsible for the success or failure of that goal than anyone else

- All the Decision Makers are expected to consider the status of all of the goals when deciding what work is carried out

Again, a tiny set of rules that achieves everything needed. Working this way means the decisions we make on what work is carried out are made within the context of everything the company is trying to achieve. We have a complete and accurate picture of how the company is performing, and we can direct our energy accordingly, in a completely agile way. All the Decision Makers in our company effectively form a small unit, regardless of their functional expertise. We sometimes talk about what we're going to do next on Slack, sometimes we get together and talk things through in person, or sometimes someone will just decide to do something and let the rest of us know later. Everybody is free to use their judgement to decide which things they think will help us achieve any and all of our goals. If I feel the need to steer us more towards one goal than another, then I get involved, but I'm just part of that decision making process. I'm not the keeper of it.

This approach removes the traditional safety rules that ensure all the goals get enough focus, but it doesn't actually expose us to any real risk. Because each goal has a representative, we are all always aware if a particular goal is at risk of failing, or needs more attention. As I mentioned, the representative for each goal is no more or less responsible for it being achieved than anyone else is. It isn't 'their' goal. What they are responsible for is understanding it and sharing information about it with everyone else. They track what work is being done to achieve it, they gather the data that measures how it's progressing, and they communicate all of that to the rest of the Decision Makers. They tell us how confident they are that the goal will be achieved, and anything else they think we might need to know to help us all make good decisions. Put simply, they're a representative for that goal. What happens in practice is that every now and then we'll get a heads up from a representative who will simply say, "If we don't give this goal some more attention, I don't think it will be achieved". We can then decide to take that onboard or not. Either way, the success or failure of that goal will be our collective responsibility.

Back when I first came up with this approach, I achieved this with daily stand-ups. The Decision Makers would get together each morning and give each other updates on the status of the goals we represented. That worked fine, but it isn't the most efficient way. Today, we use an internal tool to collect and share that information with everyone, but regardless of how it's achieved, as long as the Decision Makers have all the information about how the goals are progressing, that's enough of a safety net to ensure division of responsibility is no longer necessary.

A more complicated problem to solve is ensuring we actually make good decisions. Obviously it's of no benefit to anyone if we all run off making decisions without any thought or care for the consequences. However, the principles of Minimum Effective Management call for me not to expect people to prove every idea they have is a good one before they're allowed to act, and to give people as much autonomy as possible. So, how do you give people decision making autonomy, but still ensure you make more good decisions than bad? Much like with the problem of getting people from one side of the ravine to the other, you don't control how they do it. Instead, you put up a safety net to protect them when they do it badly. The default position is to assume people will make a good decision, not a bad one.

This is where I use data. But I use it at the end of the process, not the beginning. Instinctively, the way you'd think to use data to help with decision making would be to require data to support each decision before you make it. But as I said earlier, this can limit creativity. The way I work inverts this. Instead of asking people to justify each of their decisions with data and evidence, I keep data on the decisions they make and track how often they make good ones.

When one of my Decision Makers wants to do something, they can just do it. I would like them to be as informed as possible before they make a decision, but to be honest their process has nothing to do with me, and I stay out of it. They can use data if they want to, or they can just guess. It's not important to me. What is important to me is how often they are right. If they can keep making good decisions, I couldn't care less how they're making them. If they're doing it through reading tea leaves, through the world's most complex data modelling, or through rolling dice, it doesn't matter to me in the slightest. I just want them to be right.

So whenever someone wants to make a decision, I don't ask them to justify it, I ask them to tell me what they expect will happen as a result of the decision they're making. I then keep track of the predictions people make, and I compare them to what actually does go on to happen. Over not much time at all, that data shows me - in a way that can't be gamed or cheated - how much leeway I can give each of my Decision Makers.

If you work for me, and you have a great track record of accurately predicting what will happen as a result of the choices you make, then I don't give your choices too much scrutiny. If your judgement has been consistently sound, why should I waste both of our time making you explain to me how you make your decisions? Even if you have no data to back up what you believe, the data *I* have on *you* means I can feel comfortable trusting you. If however your predictions have consistently been wrong, and you come to me and say, "Hey, I'm going to do this really time consuming and expensive project. I don't have any evidence to support it", that's probably going to be different. In that situation, I will want to talk more about it. I'll ask you to convince me, and that might mean you providing me some supporting evidence before you can go ahead.

Instead of the safety rules that control each individual decision, I have a safety net that catches the people who aren't making good decisions. I don't care how good anyone is at measuring the past - I care how good they are at shaping the future. And when someone isn't able to shape the future the way they're trying to, my safety net catches those people and I can focus all my management energy on helping and supporting them. In the meantime, my good decision makers are running with the ball. They're getting the goals achieved and I often have no idea what they're even up to. I spend my time working with the people who will benefit from my attention. I can help them with whatever they need, and I have a lot of time to do that because I'm not managing all the people who don't need any managing.

The way I execute this is quite basic. I'm actually quite lazy so it's probably not even the best way, it's just the way I find easiest. Whenever we decide on a piece of work to do, I ask everyone who has been involved in the discussion to make some predictions on what they think will happen as a result of the decision. I usually focus on things like the specific impact people expect it will have on our key results, or the amount of time they think it will take to deliver. I make a note of what everyone says, and later on, once the dust has settled after the project is completed, I compare our predictions to what actually did end up happening. I maintain a running score for each of us, where we lose points for being wrong, and gain them for being right. I've kind of turned it into a stupid game which is far from an exact science, but it does what I need it to. There were some unexpected benefits to this approach too. I remember when I first started doing this, I had a guy on our team who was really talented, but extremely negative. Whenever we talked about doing anything even a bit risky, he would predict a catastrophe. His negativity could often derail us as we would be dragged into conversations that probably weren't needed, and his lack of confidence could become infectious. After a few months of tracking our predictions though, I was able to point him to his track record of being mostly wrong whenever he said something was going to be a disaster. Actually seeing this changed his attitude and behaviour in ways that countless managers - including me - had failed to do up until that point.

Using data in this way doesn't restrict us. It doesn't mean we can't act on instinct if we're sure about doing something that we can't prove is a good idea. But it also means that we can track how good we are at making decisions, and it reigns us back in if we're making too many bad ones. If we're acting on instinct and not getting the results we expect, then we increase the burden of proof before we make decisions. But if we're getting the results we need even without being strict about supporting evidence, then we can just be happy that things are going to plan and keep moving.

It gives us a combination of freedom, and control.

Maintainers

How I manage the relationship to goals for the Maintainers is much simpler, and in fact I've already described the approach when I explained the group recognition principle earlier on. People who have this relationship to the goals are usually part of a team of people who are handling recurring work. If you are a Customer Service Agent, for example, you will handle customer service requests each day. That's pretty much the only direction we need to give you in terms of your goals. The work itself will obviously change daily based on the specific requests you receive, but in terms of what you are tasked with by the company, you are simply asked to handle requests from our customers. There is no need for us to complicate that, and certainly not through specific goal setting.

As with the team I described in my earlier example, I do not give Maintainers individual targets and goals. Instead, they are simply asked to help achieve all the company goals as best they can, and then all performance data is made available for them to view. This creates the social incentives that drive people to perform in a way that is far more effective than any individual goal setting will ever be. People are motivated to be seen as a productive member of their team who is helping the company achieve its true purpose, and there has never been any reason for me to provide more specific goals to anyone who works in this way.

End result

This minimal approach achieves everything that goal setting is supposed to achieve, but it requires only a fraction of the effort, and there is none of the pitfalls. I've found that this approach has created a far more collective spirit. We are all genuinely working to achieve the same things, so although we all have a sense of autonomy, we're also all part of a collective effort. We're not just masters of our own small towns, we're integral parts of the whole kingdom, working together to achieve the exact same things. Instead of acting like a bunch of individual Power Rangers running around doing our own thing, we now work like we're Megazord, the giant Power Ranger that gets formed when they all come together.

Shut up, you're the geek!

Key Points

- Everyone works to achieve the company goals, rather than being set cascaded or aligned individual or team goals

- We have three different relationships with goals - Decision Makers, Implementers, and Maintainers

- We don't ask people to justify every decision they make, but we do track how good they are at making decisions

I JUST DON'T
DO IT AT ALL

Choosing who does what

Traditionally, managers have decided who works on what. That's always been the way of it. Whilst this has given us control, it has also been the ultimate 'swallow the fly' move. Most of the rest of our job is caused by taking this action. When we take on the responsibility for assigning work, we generate a huge number of follow up tasks that require a lot of skill, time and effort to complete. We solve this fairly simple initial problem in the most obvious way to us - control and authority - without considering other possibilities, and as a result we create problems that are far harder and more time consuming to solve. We also prevent our employees getting almost all of the things they want from work. By controlling what people work on and assigning them specific tasks, we take away their autonomy, their ability to control how they grow and develop their skills, and often their connection to the true company purpose.

For a manager to delegate work effectively, we have to have a genuine understanding of the skills and behaviours of each of our people. We have to know what they want and don't want to work on. We have to know who they work well with, who they clash with, and even what their current mood is. We have to team build carefully to ensure people are compatible, we have to manage conflict, manage frustration, and manage resource availability. Once again, of course it's possible to do all of this and organise people accordingly, but the scope for failure is massive. We get it wrong a lot. These are all incredibly time consuming tasks with a high failure rate, so none of them can play a part in the Minimum Effective Management approach.

Instead of trying to find a way to do those things more effectively, I just don't do them at all. And to avoid doing them, I just don't swallow the fly.

In the Minimum Effective Management workplace, managers no longer decide what work people do. Everyone decides that for themselves. Consider the work menu I described earlier. Our Decision Makers create that work menu, and our Implementers look at the menu and offer to help deliver the things they think they can help with. The Decision Makers then choose whoever they think is the most suitable out of the people who have applied. That's the process. As a result, the managers don't have to solve any of the problems that controlling those decisions can create.

- We don't need to know who works well together and who doesn't, because people can work with whoever they choose to work with

- We don't need to know which skills each one of our staff wants to develop, because people can choose what skills they work with themselves

- We don't need to know what projects they want to be involved with, because people can apply to work on whatever they want to work on

We no longer need to spend any time at all ensuring we fully understand the specific needs and preferences of our staff. On the surface that might sound like we're dismissing the things they want and need, but it's anything but that. What we're doing is giving them autonomy to address their own needs. This is better for all of us, as they are far better positioned to meet those needs than their managers ever were. As a manager, my focus was previously always divided over the needs of all my staff, the needs of the rest of the business, and of course my own needs. But I was also the gatekeeper to them doing what they wanted to do. This meant for them to have their needs met, a guy who had countless other things to focus on had to understand those needs and then act accordingly. I did my best to get that right as often as possible, but nobody will get that right all the time. I've removed that impediment now, and they get to control their own working experience.

The management role in our workplace is now very different when it comes to the work people take on. We mostly now just support and guide people in the choices they make, and the way they approach their work. Sometimes we might ask someone to do something they might not have chosen to do otherwise, but we're always just asking them. The choice remains theirs. If they have problems with their work, with their colleagues, or with their development, they might decide to talk those problems over with their manager, but we don't control the decisions they make. We're just there to help them. In many cases people aren't really sure what they want to do next, or they don't have a preference, so they just ask for something to be suggested to them. In those cases we do it, but the freedom to choose is always theirs.

How we deliver it

When I used to delegate work to people myself, there were a whole host of things I would have to take into account. I would consider their skills, and the skills other people had. I would consider their preferences, and who they worked well with. I would consider what work they'd previously done, and whether or not I'd given them the shitty end of the stick a few too many times recently. I'd even consider what their current state of mind was. I considered all of that for all of my staff, then I tried to organise them all around what I understood those things to be. I got it right a pretty decent amount of time all things considered. In fact, I used to consider it to be one of my strongest skills as a manager. But I still got it wrong often enough.

And guess who has a far better understanding of all those criteria? It's the people themselves. I was performing a matchmaking service that I didn't need to be involved with. If I had just got out of the way, everyone was more than capable of coupling themselves up with the right work for them without me being involved.

The way I meet this requirement now is far simpler. We effectively approach delegation within the company in an identical manner to hiring an external freelancer. We treat each Implementer as a freelancer with skills to offer, and each Decision Maker as someone with a job they're looking to hire a freelancer for. The only difference is that we all work together already. To do this, we just need to ensure that:

- **Implementers** are able to see the tasks to be done, the skills they require, and who is already involved

- **Decision Makers** are able to find people who have the

skills required to carry out the work that needs to be done

By exposing that information to everyone, I allow them to self-organise. Managers never have to learn what their staff need, understand their particular behaviours, or be totally up to date on their knowledge, skills, preferences and mood. We just don't swallow the fly that would lead to us needing to know all that.

The way we ensure that information is available to everyone is through technology. Each employee maintains a skills profile that is available and searchable to everyone else in the company. Decision Makers can then search for people who have the skills required to complete the work they want done.

We also have a central job board - which we call Things to Do - where Decision Makers can post requests for people to complete the work that needs doing. Implementers can then apply to work on the things that interest them.

The technology required to do this is no different to any freelance job finding app. We use an internal tool, but there are countless SaaS options out there.

This approach is simple and effective when things go to plan, but obviously it has also removed all the safety rules that traditional management depends on to stop things going wrong. We don't control what people are working on, so obviously people might end up not working at all. Also, some tasks might not get done as people might not be willing or able to do them. So, we need a safety net. We need to make sure we catch those events so we can handle them.

To keep things compartmentalised, I'm not going to address the quality of people's work here (I have a method for managing performance which I'll explain later). This safety net is simply concerned with ensuring people *are* working, and that specific tasks don't get ignored. It needs to catch the situations where either someone isn't picking up any work at all, or where a piece of work isn't being done because nobody will pick it up.

Making sure people are working

Let's start with catching if someone isn't picking up work. This is very simple. An important thing to note is that we don't need our safety net to tell us *why* someone isn't picking up work - that's our job to determine as their managers. The safety net just needs to catch the people who aren't picking up work, for whatever reason, and bring it to our attention. It might be that they're being lazy, it might be that they don't have any skills that people need, it might be that people aren't choosing to work with them. Whatever the reason someone falls in the safety net, it doesn't matter. We can speak to them and find out the reasons, as long as we know it's happening. And because we save so much time not worrying about delegating work to every single person, we're able to focus as much time as we need to on working with those people.

All that's needed to achieve this is a way of seeing at a glance what people are working on, and more importantly, if someone isn't working on anything. We use our internal tool to highlight any team member who isn't currently working on anything to the rest of us through a central dashboard. Again though, any number of SaaS products could meet this need.

This safety net also takes into account another Minimum Effective Management principle; group recognition. If someone isn't working on anything, it isn't just their manager who can see that, it's everyone. Everyone in the company can see what everyone else is working on, and when people aren't working on anything at all, that is visible to everyone. This isn't to shame them, and there's no requirement for anyone to be working on anything. They make their own choices and they can do nothing at all if they want. However, if they aren't working, their coworkers will see that they aren't working. They can make the choice, but they also have to own it.

This is something I will probably over stress throughout the book - Minimum Effective Management isn't a magic wand that solves all my management problems for me. The human part of the job is still very much mine to do. Once my safety net catches the people who aren't working - whatever the reason for that is - this is where I have to earn my keep as a manager to try to fix that. This is where my coaching, my feedback and my performance management can add value (see the *resources* section for more information on these things). Minimum Effective Management doesn't do that stuff for me or make me any better at doing it - but it does buy me vast amounts of time by letting me focus my energy only on the people who actually need that kind of support.

Making sure work is picked up

The other thing I need to make sure we catch is when specific work isn't being picked up. Again, the reason why it isn't being picked up doesn't matter. As long as we know it's happening, we can then find out the reasons for that ourselves. This is even simpler to handle than ensuring people are working, and it doesn't require any technology at all. If the Decision Maker who is running a project can't find someone to do some work needed for it, then we talk about it. It's no more complicated than that. We might find out that we have a skills shortage, or that people don't believe in the goal or the project itself. We might find out that people don't like working with some of the other people involved with the project, or that they don't like working in that area of the business. Whatever the reason, we always find it out quickly, and we're always better off for knowing. With traditional management, problems such as the ones I just listed can sometimes go undetected for months or even years. People don't necessarily talk about the problems, because the safety rules we put in place force them to work around them, even if doing so creates an unhealthy or unproductive working environment. We assign someone work, and they don't mention that they hate it, that they don't believe in it, that it doesn't interest them, or that they don't like working with the person running the project. They don't mention it because they don't want to appear difficult. The problems never get out in the open, and they never get resolved. By letting these problems play out instead of preventing them, we bring them front and center so we can then resolve them. If we have a skills shortage, we can train or hire. If certain people are clashing, we can work on conflict resolution. If nobody wants to work in a particular area of the business, we can find out why and address it. No matter what the reasons turn out to be, everyone is better off for having those reasons out in the open.

Key Points

- We let people choose what they work on, and who they work with

- We have a safety net that catches the people who don't pick up work. We focus our management energy on those people and let the others get on with it

- We have a safety net that catches when specific work isn't being picked up, which prompts us to identify and address the reasons for that

HOPEFULLY I'LL JUST BE ON FIRE

Staying up to date

If there was one activity that I felt absolutely no hesitation at all in excluding from Minimum Effective Management, it was recurring meetings. I was never really sure that they added any value, and frankly I hated them. I really hated them. A lot.

Sometimes I worry about what will happen when I die. According to most of the popular religions, I'll not be going to the good place. And if there is a hell, my personal one will be an eternity spent in recurring meetings. I'll have to listen to someone talk about all the things they did last week that don't affect me, while someone else asks inane questions that nobody needs the answers to, peppering each sentence with increasingly irritating buzzwords. I'll sit there screaming inside, praying for the sweet release of oblivion, but it will never come. Sometimes I'll plead with them all to let me leave so I can actually do some work, and I'll be rounded on and told I'm being unprofessional by someone who just invented 20 new ways to say absolutely nothing. If the universe is a cruel and terrible place, this will be my eternity. Hopefully I'll just be on fire.

Thankfully, while I occupy this mortal form, I don't have

to suffer recurring meetings anymore, because even before I came up with Minimum Effective Management, I had banned them all. When I first decided to do this, nobody was onboard. I wanted to ditch everything - one-on-ones, scrum ceremonies, departmental meetings - the lot. Although everyone agreed that the meetings were dreadful and taking up too much time, they were convinced they were a necessary evil. After a lot of persuading, and in spite of their doubts, eventually everyone agreed to disagree with me but commit anyway. We agreed we'd stop having recurring meetings, on the condition that if everything was a disaster, we'd just start having them again. The worst thing that could happen was a couple of weeks of disruption, and things weren't going so well that that would have made a big difference anyway. That was Monday. By Wednesday, we'd unblocked everything that had been blocked, the right people were having the right conversations at the right time, and I no longer wanted to kill myself and everyone around me.

Recurring meetings are a lot like cigarettes. One of the things smokers believe is that smoking reduces stress. I used to be a smoker and believed this myself. If I was stressed and I had a cigarette, I felt less stressed. However, what you fail to realise as a smoker is that the stress you are eliminating is the stress of needing a cigarette. When you're addicted to nicotine, the withdrawal feels remarkably similar to stress, so when you have a cigarette you alleviate this feeling and believe you have reduced your stress. But if you just didn't smoke, you'd have felt less stressed the entire time, not just when you finally got to have a cigarette. Smoking does not reduce stress for a non-smoker, far from it. In his excellent book *The Easy Way to Stop Smoking*, Allen Carr equates this to wearing an unbearably tight pair of shoes all day, just to feel the relief of taking them off for five minutes once every couple of hours.

With recurring meetings, we fall into exactly the same trap. The recurring meeting blocks communication for a whole week while we wait for the time we're allowed to talk to each other, then it finally unblocks us when we get in the meeting room, and we think the meeting helped us. We've parked things that we really could have just talked about right away, so by the time the meeting comes around everyone has a huge amount to discuss, and we all think, "God, how would we cope without this meeting!?". The truth is that the meeting caused the problem. Conversations that would have allowed work to progress have happened far too late, decisions that could have been made right away have been delayed, and work hasn't been done that absolutely could have been done. The meeting is only solving a problem that the very existence of the meeting created.

The recurring meeting is yet another boiling frog solution that persists from an age when we didn't have a better way. When we didn't have the technology to allow a group of people to share information between one another quickly and efficiently whenever they wanted no matter where they were in the world, the most sensible way to organise would have been to schedule a recurring meeting. We couldn't realistically have rounded everyone up every single time someone needed to discuss something, so we accepted that the only way to work was to have a scheduled time and place where we'd all get together to discuss things. That's no longer necessary. Technology allows us to have these group conversations on the fly. We do it every day already. Most of us interact with several different Teams or Slack channels daily. We don't need to schedule a time we all have those conversations, we just throw information into them when we want to say something, and we read the information they contain when we're free to take it in. It's easy, it's something we're all doing anyway, and it really should have signalled the death of the recurring meeting. But it didn't, most companies still have huge numbers of these meetings. When I've been asked to help clients improve their efficiency, I almost always find that everyone attends at least one recurring meeting nearly every single day. This is destroying their productivity for two reasons. Firstly, it means people's time is far too structured, forcing people to think about things at specific times instead of allowing them to just dynamically focus their energy where it's most needed. Secondly, it constantly disrupts people from their flow state, preventing them ever building any momentum, which for a lot of jobs in a modern company is essential to delivering good work.

One of the big push backs people gave me when I first decided to abolish recurring meetings was that they believed it would be impossible to get enough time from one another. "Hannah is always so busy", I kept hearing, "I need to get time booked in or I'll never get to talk to her". But as it turned, out Hannah was only so busy and difficult to get hold of because she was constantly in recurring meetings. Once she didn't have those meetings, people were able to contact her whenever they needed her, and she still ended up with far more free time. Getting rid of those meetings immediately allowed her to have far more conversations that actually needed to happen, as and when they needed to happen, instead of spending most of her day sitting in meetings listening to conversations she didn't need to be involved with. Nobody ever had a problem getting hold of Hannah, or anyone else. What we overlook with these recurring meetings is that most attendees really don't need to be involved in the majority of the conversations that go on in them. In any given two hour session, most of the attendees are probably only really needed for about 15 minutes of what goes on in there. The rest of the time they're just sitting there questioning their life choices and trying to look like they're paying attention as they wait for something that concerns them to come up. Given that people are often spending half their days in recurring meetings, that's a lot of wasted time. And that's not even factoring in one of the biggest ways that recurring meetings kill our momentum. It's not just the time they take, it's the time all around them as well.

When someone has a meeting scheduled for 3pm, guess what happens before and after that meeting? Almost certainly nothing. The chances of getting any high quality work done after lunch and before that meeting are really low. Sometimes it might happen, but generally people aren't even going to try. And after the meeting, it's nearly home time so they might as well not kick anything off. If you drag 10 people into that meeting, that's 40 hours of working time you just throw away.

That's just the one meeting. Add up your one-on-ones, your departmental meetings, your steering groups, your all hands, and all the other meetings you have to go to, and at the end of it you're left with almost no time for any actual work to take place. When your job is creative - which the majority of jobs in a modern company are in some way or another - the most valuable thing you can have is an uninterrupted block of time. Recurring meetings strip these opportunities to almost nothing. I frequently work with clients where none of the employees has the chance to work a full day uninterrupted. The value that can be gained from changing that is almost immeasurable. A guy I know once told me that his biggest challenge at work was "trying to find a few minutes to actually do my job". I've repeated that to so many people and seen it resonate depressingly often.

These recurring meetings are safety rules. I couldn't even guess how many meetings I've been asked to attend over my career where the purpose of the meeting was just to "make sure we're all on the same page". On the other side of the coin - the recurring meetings I have organised myself - these have nearly always been so I could keep informed about what people were doing, or to give them a chance to talk to me about anything that might have been on their mind. All of these things are precautionary - we're having meetings in case there is something we need to talk about. In other words - we're using a meeting to find out if we need to have a meeting.

So, as you may have guessed, recurring meetings are not a part of Minimum Effective Management. I still have meetings, but I don't have them as a default. Meetings only happen if they need to happen, and I use something other than the meeting itself to determine if that's the case.

I've found the approach I use for this easiest to explain when I just show what the output of it is. Let me use a simplified example. Assume I have just three staff, and I want to identify if I need to have a conversation with any of them about what they're working on.

To enable me to do this, I ask each of them to send me a quick message each morning in which they give me an estimate of how many more days it will take them to finish what they're working on. Nothing more than that. I don't need an explanation or justification, just the estimate. I keep track of those estimates, but I don't expect them to be flawlessly accurate and nobody is ever hauled over the coals for getting them wrong. I just always want to know whatever their latest best estimate is for when their work will be delivered.

Now, let's say it's Wednesday morning, and I have received all of their estimates each day so far this week. This is what they look like:

ESTIMATED DAYS REMAINING

	Mon	Tue	Wed
Mark	7	6	5
Anna	10	9	8
Chris	5	6	10

Mark and Anna's work seems to be progressing fine, right? The estimated number of days they think they need is going down each day. But on Monday, Chris said he thought he'd be finished in five days, and today he's saying he thinks it'll be ten days. Based on this, I know I might need to talk to Chris to find out if he's got a problem. I can leave Mark and Anna alone as everything seems to be going according to plan with them. But I might go and talk to Chris.

If I only have three direct reports, this approach saves me having two status update conversations that I don't need to have. But I've used this approach to manage as many as 40 direct reports, and I was still able to easily ensure everything stayed on track. Even with so many people to support, the conversations I had were high quality and never rushed.

There were rarely more than a couple of people each day who needed my attention, so I was able to focus on them completely. I never once had a status update conversation I didn't need to have, which meant I had all the time and energy necessary for the ones I did need to have.

The key to making this work is that I look at the trend of where the estimates are heading. In the example above I used a three day trend to keep it simple, but I generally look at the trend over the previous five days. Everyone can have a day or two where their estimate jumps up, and that doesn't really matter to me too much. What's important to me is that over a few days the trend is on the way down. I have found that as long as I pay attention to that trend, I can't go too far wrong. Each day I can easily identify the people I might need to talk to, and I can leave everyone else alone. Obviously there are exceptions to this, but I can just use my judgement in each case. For example, if your estimate jumps from 1 day to 20 days overnight, I'm probably going to talk to you right away regardless of the trend up to that point.

I just use a shared Google sheet to collect these estimates, as that way I don't have to do much work to keep it all organised and view any emerging trends. It makes it really easy for me to see the people that might need my attention just by looking at the sheet each morning once everyone has made their updates. Again though, how the estimates are gathered and displayed doesn't really matter. As long as I have the information, I can identify the meetings I might need to have without having the meeting just to be sure.

To be clear, these status updates are not a replacement for the conversations. I still have those conversations if and when they need to happen. What's particularly powerful about this approach is that there's really no way that anyone can game it. Some of the more cynical managers I've explained this to have been concerned that people would just say their estimate was going down each day, even if they weren't really getting anywhere. That doesn't actually matter though.

Let's take a worst case scenario. Let's say you work for me, and you've taken on a task. You initially estimated it would take you ten days, and each day you've dropped the estimate by a day to show that it's progressing. However, you haven't really been doing any work at all. You've just been sitting at home watching Netflix. What are your options as this plays out? How do you get away with this? What do you do when the day it needs to be delivered is approaching? You're either going to have to suddenly up the estimate, or you're going to have to do the work and catch up. There is no way to hide. If you've just been outright lying and not doing the work, and all of a sudden you push the estimate back up to ten days, that's going to prompt a conversation with me, and I'm going to immediately find out what you did. What's far more likely - and I'm fairly sure is what actually does happen in my company all the time - is that you'll find a way to get the work done without having to drastically bump that estimate up. I suspect people who work for me often take days where they coast and don't do much, but they then make up the time later on. They might try and game it, and they might be able to squeeze a few days out here and there, but in the end they're going to have to just do the work. There's no getting away from it. And as long as the work gets done, what do I care? In fact, I actually want people to be able to work in this way. I want people to work around their natural rhythms. I know that the way I work is very rarely linear. I don't work 8 hours a day. My average over a 7 day period is probably 8 hours a day, but within that 7 days there are days where I do almost nothing, and other days where I might work 20 hours. It's just how I am. I know I'm more effective if I don't have to fight my natural pattern, and I don't want the people who work for me to have to do that either. Whatever their pattern is, I'm happy for them to work to it as long as they still get the work done roughly when we planned for.

The other potential trick someone could pull is estimating something taking much longer to deliver than they think it actually will, in order to buy themselves more time to relax. As it turns out, this isn't something that seems to happen. The reason for this is that the economic and social incentives drive people not to do it. If you're consistently putting in big estimates that are much higher than your colleagues, everyone you work with can see that. It will make you less likely to be picked to do work you want to do because the Decision Makers will see that you don't deliver things promptly. Also, very few people want the people they work with to think that they're slow, so even if there are people in my team dishonest enough to want to use this trick, they don't seem to be doing it. And even if they do one day - I can see their estimates. There's nothing to stop me talking to them and challenging something I don't think is realistic.

This approach means any meetings I have are always in response to specific events. We don't have any more "make sure we're on the same page" meetings. We stay connected using Slack, we make decisions when we need to make decisions, and if someone thinks we need to get together, they arrange that and we do. I don't attend a single recurring meeting, whether in person or via video chat. We talk when we need to talk. We say only what we need to say, and we only say it to the people who need to hear it.

Key Points

- We gather daily estimates in order to forecast when things will be delivered without having recurring progress update meetings or stand-ups

- We use the trend of those daily estimates to identify who we might need to have detailed conversations with

- We never have any recurring meetings. We all arrange meetings as and when we need them, and we share information on the fly using whatever tool works best

THERE'S NO CHANCE I'M DOING THAT!

Organising people

Thankfully most companies have moved, or are at least moving, towards a less controlling way of working already. There is certainly more freedom given to people when it comes to things like working from home than there ever has been before, and this was happening even before we faced a global pandemic that made it mandatory. However, I believe an even greater benefit can be gained by removing all of the expectations we have of people regarding when, where and how they work. Before I get going, I should acknowledge that I probably take this a bit further than most managers would be comfortable to go right away. If you read what I do and think to yourself, "there's no chance I'm doing that", don't worry. It's unlikely to get in the way of taking on the rest of the approach. I'll share the way I do it, and why I think it's the best way, but I don't think this is a binary choice between giving people complete autonomy and retaining complete control. There's a spectrum of freedom. I believe that the more freedom you can give people the better, but you don't need to do all of it right away. In truth I can't actually remember how I got to where I am with this, but I'm fairly sure I did it in stages. I didn't jump from standard management controls, straight to the approach I use today.

My approach today is to give people absolute and total control of how, when, where and even if they work. Nobody that works for me ever has to ask to be anywhere. Everyone makes their own choices. Approval for these choices is not required. They don't have a vacation allowance - they can take as much time off as they want to take. They don't have set hours - they can work whenever they want to work for however long they want to work. They don't have individual responsibilities or job descriptions either. In fact, they don't have any expectations placed on them at all beyond one simple and universal job description that every employee is given regardless of their role:

"Use your best judgement to help us achieve our goals"

That's it. That is the complete job description of every employee who ever works for me. This has proven to be immeasurably more effective than any management I have ever seen carried out.

My staff are responsible for helping us achieve our goals. I keep track of if they are doing that or not. As long as they are, all the other expectations that are typically placed on employees become arbitrary. Most of the traditional expectations we have of people at work aren't really things we actually want or need from them - they're things we think they need to do in order for us to get what we really want.

Do we really want people in the office? Or do we just believe that if they don't come to the office they might not work as effectively, and if they don't work as effectively then we won't achieve what we're trying to achieve. When we expect people to come to the office, aren't we really just trying to make sure they help us achieve our goals?

Do we really benefit from them being available between 9am - 5pm? Or do we believe that they need to be available between those hours in order to make sure people can collaborate. And don't we just want them to collaborate because if they can't do that it would make it harder for them to help us achieve our goals?

Ultimately, expectations like this aren't necessary. Not in the end. I no longer set any of these foundation expectations. I think about the reason I'm considering setting a specific rule, and I follow the logic of it until I find the thing I really want to achieve by setting that rule. When I do that, I always end up with the same answer - I want them to help us achieve our goals.

The following thought experiment helped me decide on this approach. I imagined that through blind luck, I happened to employ an all-powerful Genie who was able to magically achieve all my goals with a click of his fingers, the moment I asked him to. (You're totally picturing the Genie from Aladdin, and that's fine). I then imagined that this Genie insisted on never coming into the office, and would only work whenever he wanted to work, wherever he wanted to work. Then I asked myself if I would care. The answer is that of course I wouldn't. I wouldn't care one bit where or when or for how long he worked, as long as he achieved my goals for me. So why should I care about that stuff when it comes to my employees?

I have explained this approach to people before and seen a look of dread spread across their face. The question that follows is always in the ballpark of, "you can't seriously be saying that we should let people not bother to work, can you?"

In theory, yes I am. But in practice, I'm not at all. Not unless they actually are an all-powerful Genie. I expect my employees to help us achieve our goals, and I make sure I know if they're doing that. If them coming into the office is something that's necessary for them to help achieve our goals, then they're going to end up having to come into the office whether I specifically tell them to do it or not. If working 8 hours a day at the same time other people are working is necessary in order for them to help us achieve our goals, then they will end up doing that too. The only things they will be able to get away with not doing are things that aren't actually necessary in order for our goals to be achieved. So in other words - they're things that shouldn't matter to me. Unfortunately, I have yet to employ the all-powerful Genie who has been able to help me achieve all our goals without doing any work. But I'm open to it, and my rules don't forbid it.

I really believe that treating people this way is crucial to creating a workplace they will thrive in. Most people don't want this level of freedom out of a desire to exploit it and be lazy, they want it because they want to use their judgement and work when and where it makes the most sense. When we make people ask for permission to do something, we're taking their responsibility away. If someone asks me for the day off, and I say yes, the consequences of them taking that day off are on me. This means they are actually more likely to try to take a day off that they know would be inconvenient because it takes away the moral and social incentives. If I give them permission, it's not their fault if it causes a problem, it's mine. But if I don't make them ask me, any problems their absence causes are their responsibility, not mine. And guess what, if I don't take that responsibility away from them, they usually act responsibly.

When we don't take their sense of responsibility away, and instead we just ask them to make sure their choices don't cause problems for the people they work with, I've found that they are almost universally responsible about it. And if they're not, this is immediately made clear to everyone. If someone just does whatever they want to do regardless of how it affects everyone else, we can all see that. This brings me to the other benefit of this approach - it effortlessly shows me something that many companies spend a fortune trying to measure. It shows me who is engaged, and who isn't. It's an extremely powerful tool that tells me more than any employee engagement survey ever could. Want to see if people are engaged? Tell them they can do whatever they want, and see what they do. I don't ever have to ask anyone if they're engaged. I can actually see it. There's an old expression - don't tell me you're funny, make me laugh. Well I don't have to ask people if they think I'm funny, I can just see who's laughing.

For some reason, this specific aspect of management has always been extremely important to me. In truth, I can't 100% tell you why I feel this way. I think it just comes down to the fact that I don't believe we can or should trick people into thinking that we're treating them like adults. A lot of the time when managers ask me how to empower their employees, or provide them autonomy, what they're really asking me for is a way to make their staff *feel* empowered, whilst not having to give up any of their own power at all. They want the benefit, but they aren't willing to give up the control. What they end up doing is rarely genuine, usually transparent, and almost never achieves anything of value. I think people thrive when they feel like they are trusted equals, and the trick to making people feel that way is that there is no trick. We just have to do it. We have to actually trust them, and we have to actually treat them like equals. And that means we have to trust them to make responsible decisions about when and where they work.

There's also something very simple and undeniably true that's worth considering if this seems like a scary decision to make. It's something a lot of people seem to miss. The worst thing that can happen when you work like this is that certain people don't take the responsibility you give them seriously. That's really not a big deal. If that happens, you can deal with them individually. There is no need to treat everyone like a child because some people act like children. If you have ten employees you treat like adults, but one of them acts like a child, you don't have to change the rules for all ten people. You can just take away autonomy from the person who isn't deserving of it. You can deal with them separately. And in order to do that, you have to find out who is who by letting them all make their own choices.

Key Points

- We let people decide when and where they work

- Everyone has the same job description: "Use your best judgement to help us achieve our goals"

- Each person is responsible for communicating their plans to the people who need to know them so it doesn't cause disruption

Getting what I need - Recap

- **There are no individual goals** - Everyone works to the same goals. This creates a shared purpose and avoids creating conflicting incentives or confusion. Decision Makers, Implementers and Maintainers interact with the goals differently

- **People choose the work they do themselves** - Managers do not delegate work to people. Decision Makers advertise internally for people to pick up specific work, and Implementers can apply to do the work they want to do

- **We track estimate trends and only talk when necessary** - There is no need for any planned or recurring meetings. We use Slack and DoThings to stay connected with each other. Managers track estimate trends for all work being carried out so they can predict when things might be delivered, and identify when something may be drifting off track

- **People control their own time** - Everybody is given the same job description: "Use your best judgement to help us achieve our goals". Nobody needs to ask permission to be anywhere, and everyone is entirely responsible for the impact their choices have on their coworkers

5

PROVIDING WHAT THEY NEED

When the manager was invented, we all knew where we stood when it came to our happiness at work: our manager couldn't care less about it. It was that simple. The manager was our boss, and their job was to pay us as little as necessary to make us do exactly what they wanted us to do, regardless of what we wanted. What we wanted was irrelevant to them. They weren't our agent. They weren't ensuring we were paid fairly or making sure we were getting to work on the things that interested us. They were just our boss. I'm not saying that was better, I'm just saying we all knew where we stood. Our expectations were thoroughly managed. We expected nothing, and that's exactly what we got.

As the working world changed, employees started to have expectations of their manager. It was probably small things at first, things like, "I work 23 hours a day, could I have a lunch break?", or, "I catch fire more often than I'd like to, could you do something about that?". That kind of stuff. Begrudgingly, employers started to listen to these requests, and managers started having to consider employee needs as well as their own needs. Yadda yadda yadda for a few decades, and you have servant leadership.

I know, right. You give them an inch, they take a mile.

Now, obviously today things are much better. I'm not advocating a return to this draconian leadership style. Back when I believed in traditional management, I think my style was more closely aligned to servant leadership than any other. I believe in the philosophy of it, but I also believe there are consequences to it.

By establishing the expectation that your manager will be looking out for you in this way, we've created an ignition point that can torch the whole relationship. It's like we have our hand on the lever that controls who the trolley will hit, and we've told you that we'll make sure it doesn't hit you. But we can't always do that. Sometimes we have to let it hit you. Sometimes we have to actually redirect it so it does hit you when it wasn't going to otherwise. And because we told you we weren't going to do that, that's damaging for the relationship.

Think back to that scary manager who didn't have to worry about you at all. The boss. The boss could let the trolley hit you, and it wouldn't really change how you felt about him because he didn't tell you he was going to do anything else. And even if you did hate your boss, it didn't really matter. You didn't need a strong working relationship with your boss back then. You just had to do what he told you to do. But today, our relationship with our manager is an integral part of our job. If we're angry with our manager because we feel they haven't been looking out for us when they should have been, that often has an impact on how we actually perform.

This is a perfect example of managers instinctively solving a problem with authority and control. We realised that people wanted career development and fair pay, so we gave the manager responsibility to make sure those things were taken care of. When the manager is able to direct the trolley away from you, everything is great. We've given you an agent who has helped you, and you're happy. But when the manager has to let the trolley hit you, we've done the opposite. Rather than giving you an agent who has helped you develop your career, we've just created a blocker that has prevented you from developing it on your own. And that can destroy our working relationship.

On the surface, I appreciate that how I now approach this might suggest that I've just stopped caring about my staff and how their careers develop. I'm not saying that at all. I work the way I do now because I care deeply about what my employees get out of working for me, not because I don't. I want everyone that works for me to develop and grow exactly the way they want to develop and grow. I want them to get paid what they feel they deserve to be paid. And I've realised that they are the best people to make sure that happens, not me. If I have ten direct reports, and I'm responsible for all of their careers, all of their salaries, and all of their happiness at work, none of them will get a decent amount of my focus. Of the time I can spend thinking about all of those things for my staff, they'll each get about one tenth of it. If I'm a gatekeeper to them getting the things they want and need, there's a very good chance I'm going to hinder more than I help. But they control 100% of their own time. All I need to do is give them the tools to act on their own to pursue their own wants and needs.

NOBODY IS GIVING YOU YOUR PAY

YOU'RE EARNING IT

Salary reviews

It's not a new thought that pay isn't what really motivates people. Financial reward has been shown time and time again to not be a particularly powerful motivator. One of the reasons for this is that it's a future incentive. We could work really really hard today and possibly get a pay rise in the future. Or we could watch monkeys reacting to magic tricks on YouTube today and have fun right now. The reward of having fun is immediate, so it wins a lot of the time.

However, although our pay does not create a particularly influential positive economic incentive, it often is a reason for us to become frustrated or demotivated. You may not be able to motivate me just by paying me more, but you can certainly demotivate me by not paying me what I deserve. It's not really the money, it's the fact you aren't giving me the recognition, and the fact it's just not fair. I might not really care about the money at all, but there's still a good chance I'm going to start being difficult if I think you're not giving me what I deserve.

And this only happens because I expect you to pay me what I deserve without me asking you to. I get to the end of the year and I expect you to give me a pay rise based on my worth. I expect you to be my advocate. I walk into my pay review expecting you to reward me with a pay increase I haven't asked for simply because you have noticed I deserve it. The money you give me in that pay review will tell me exactly how much you value me, and if it's not enough, I'll feel like you don't value me at all.

The conflicting interests we create for managers really come into play here. If I'm your manager, and you expect that I'm going to act as your agent, and all my other staff expect the same, and the company expects that I'll be doing my best to keep salary costs down, then there is no correct choice I can make. I am representing too many interests, and I am always going to be acting against one of them. I have a budget, so any money I give you, I can't give to anyone else. Not to mention the fact giving you money might actually have a negative financial impact for me personally. Several times over my career I've been in a position where the lower I kept the costs of my department, the higher my bonus or overall compensation package would have been. In other words - the less I paid my staff, the more I would get paid myself. I can put my hand on my heart and say that I've never let that influence my choices, but I know for a fact that isn't the case for a lot of managers.

We exacerbate this problem with the annual pay review. When we make the pay review a guaranteed annual event for every employee, we end up giving out small pay increases to people who haven't really done anything to warrant them. The moment we carry out the review, we create a situation where giving them nothing at all would cause a problem. If you say you'll review someone's salary, then you review it and give them nothing, they will likely start to question if you're really looking out for them. You can't expect them not to find that demotivating, even in situations where they themselves can't offer a single reason they should be given an increase.

Back when I used to carry out the annual review, I would frequently find myself in situations where I didn't have the budget to give someone the increase that would reflect how I truly valued them. I used to put so much time and effort into working out how to use my allocated salary budget, but no matter how hard I tried, every salary review period would leave some people disappointed. A lot of the time that disappointment would end up directed at me. The fall out could often be long lasting or even permanent. Someone who had been trying really hard would get disheartened and stop putting in as much effort. Someone positive would turn into someone negative. Someone who used to trust me would stop trusting me.

All in all, the annual pay review is a time consuming activity that generates poor results and means we give money to the wrong people. It tacitly tells people that whether they have a good case for receiving a pay rise or not, once a year we will probably give them one anyway. The annual review connects recognition to salary, and that creates nothing but problems. Put simply, it's not got a place in Minimum Effective Management.

So I don't do annual pay reviews anymore. But that doesn't mean salary doesn't ever get reviewed. In fact, the way I work now provides the perfect environment for any employee who actually does deserve more reward.

The first thing I did when I made this change was make it completely clear to everyone that I didn't consider salary to be connected to recognition at all. I explained that I would never give anyone an unprompted pay increase, no matter how amazing I thought they were. I explained that my job as their manager was to keep the salary costs down, and that as a result it was a conflict of interest for me to be responsible for bringing their salaries up. However, I also explained that I *expected* them to come to me when they felt they had a good case for getting a pay increase. I made it very clear that I always wanted to pay them fairly, and would always listen to any case for a pay increase that anyone made. I told them that I didn't ever want any of them to be sitting around waiting for me to correct a problem with their pay that they themselves were aware of. So all they had to do when they felt they deserved a pay rise was come and talk to me and tell me why. I would always hear them out, and I would never be annoyed or think they were being demanding, even if I didn't end up agreeing with them. But I also made it clear that I would never try to correct the problem myself if they didn't bring it up. Their salary was their responsibility, not mine.

That was it. No more annual pay reviews. No more evenings sitting around playing with a budget spreadsheet working out how I could possibly keep everyone happy, and no parade of meetings handing out depressingly small increases that made no difference to anyone. No work for me at all in fact. And everyone was immediately happier and better off.

I don't place any restrictions on when these conversations can happen. It's not an annual event. Anyone can come and talk to me about their salary at any time. However, that doesn't necessarily mean that I will immediately give them any increase we might agree on. Those budget restrictions I had to work with before haven't magically gone away, so sometimes salary increases can only happen at set times. But those restrictions on when an increase can be applied don't mean that the conversations regarding pay can't happen whenever they need to happen. When the pay rise can actually be applied doesn't need to have any bearing on when it can be discussed and agreed.

Working this way actually makes budgeting for salary much easier as well. I'm never taken by surprise anymore. When we plan our budget for the year, I typically already know what pay increases I need to provide, and can let the CFO know what my final budget will be right away. I've already had all the conversations I need to have with my staff, because they've already come to me if they want an increase.

Even knowing what I know about how this works, when I explain it I still sometimes think it all seems far too simple. So here are a few reasons why it's better for everyone.

It opens doors, it doesn't close them

When you think that your manager will give you a pay rise as a way of showing recognition, you wait for them to give it to you even when you feel like you deserve it. You often don't feel like you can just ask for it. You worry you will seem demanding if you do, or sometimes you don't ask because you actually want them to offer it to you - you want the recognition you think it implies. This means that if you think you deserve an increase, but for whatever reason your manager does not, a conversation about that pay rise won't ever happen. You'll wait and wait and wait, and you'll build up resentment, and you won't get your increase or even find out why you're not getting it.

However, if you know that no matter how much your

manager values you, they won't ever offer you a pay rise, and you know that there is no annual review coming, and you know that you're actually expected to ask for a pay rise if you feel like you deserve one, then you won't feel any resentment at all. You'll put your case together, and you'll go to your manager and explain your position exactly the way you all agreed you would. Your manager can then agree or disagree with you, and either way the outcome for both parties will be better.

There are three potential outcomes to that conversation.

The simplest one is that they agree that you deserve a pay rise, and be able to commit to giving it to you. Great. Problem solved. Back to work.

Alternatively, they might not agree you deserve a pay rise. If that's the case, then at least you'll have had the conversation and will know where you stand. If it was their responsibility to review your pay and give you a pay rise, you'd have been waiting for them to come and talk to you, or waiting for your annual review, whilst either getting frustrated or building up false expectations. But your manager would have had no way of knowing that you felt like you deserved a pay rise, and by the time they found out, the damage would have been done. You'd already be annoyed. But when you're responsible for initiating the conversation, even if they don't accept your case, you can find out exactly what you need to do to secure the increase you want. This is a much better outcome than if you'd not had the conversation.

The other possibility is that they agree you deserve an increase, but they aren't able to meet your expectations at that time, for whatever reasons. And if that's the case, you knowing where you stand can only be a good thing. If you work for a company that can't match your ambition, it's better to know that than not.

No matter what the outcome of the conversation is, it is always far better if the person responsible for initiating that conversation is the person who wants the pay rise.

It makes people consider their value

When your manager is responsible for giving you a raise, you really don't have to think too much about your contribution in detailed terms. You can just sit back and think, "Yeah, I'm pretty ace", and wait for your manager to recognise this and give you all your money. But when you have to make the case yourself, you really have to think about the impact you make. You have to know what you can do that actually does add value so you are worth more money to the company, and you have to pay attention to your performance. It makes you aware that you are responsible for your performance, not your manager. When you have to make a case for getting a pay increase, it will encourage you to always know and do the things that add the most value.

The effect of this has been significant. When be began working this way people suddenly became far more aware of their performance. It was like it had flipped a switch in their heads, and they began making connections between their behaviour and their reward that they hadn't been making before. It also made people far more reasonable. A number of people who I knew had a track record of grumbling to each other about pay stopped doing that. The moment they actually had to make a detailed case for being paid more, they realised they couldn't really justify it. At the same time, it now felt kind of stupid to complain to their coworkers about pay, given that everyone knew that it was entirely in their hands whether they got a pay rise or not.

It saves time

If you manage salary this way, salary reviews will take up almost none of your time. There isn't an annual review for every single employee regardless of the situation, there is only a salary review if an employee requests one. And this means that the only reviews you're ever going to carry out will have been prepared by the person who requested it. They are reviewing their salary, not you.

Every problem I had with pay reviews went away when I started to work like this. I don't ever have resentful employees who feel they aren't appreciated, because I make it clear that pay increases aren't how I show my appreciation.

Acknowledging that I can't be their advocate in this regard doesn't show them that I don't care about them or that I'm trying to pay them unfairly - quite the opposite. It shows them that I want things to be completely fair. It shows them that I think their salary is important enough that the person responsible for making sure it's fair shouldn't have conflicting interests. When I introduced this, it put an end to any uncomfortable salary conversations, and any dissatisfaction about salary went away with it as well. Obviously I was happier that it made my life easier, but that's not the real reason I value this approach so highly. The real reason is that it truly treats people as equals. Salary reviews with a manager offering salary as reward or recognition always felt childish to me. I can think of very few annual reviews I've been given that matched my expectations, and I'd always walk out feeling a little patronised, even on the occasions I'd got what I wanted. I think that's because the dynamic is inherently unbalanced. The boss gives, the employee receives. But it shouldn't be like that. Nobody is giving you your pay. You're earning it. You shouldn't have to feel grateful for it. You go to work and you contribute, and that contribution has value. You should be treated as an adult who is able to determine your own value. As your manager, I should be the person you can negotiate that with, not the authority figure handing out small increases like they're gold stars.

Bonus payments

We also operate a bonus scheme, and I handle bonus payments in a similar but not identical way. When it's time for the bonus to be paid, I set a baseline based on our financial performance which becomes the default amount someone can expect to receive. Let's say for example the default payment is 7% of salary.

I then tell everyone that their bonus payment will be 7% of their salary, unless one of two things happens:

- I contact them to tell them that their bonus payment will actually be lower

- They contact me and ask for it to be higher

The same as with salary changes, I make it very clear that no matter how exceptional I think someone has been over the year, unless they convince me otherwise, they'll get no more than 7%. The difference is that occasionally I might believe someone deserves less than the default for some reason, and if that's the case I talk to those people to let them know why.

On the other side of the coin, if someone wants to make a

case for receiving a higher bonus, they need to tell me. But I keep this as simple as possible. Initially, they don't even need to explain their case at all. They can just message me and say, "I think my bonus should be x%". If I agree, we don't even talk about it. I make the change, and the matter is closed. However, if I don't agree, I just tell them they'll need to make a case for it, then we get together and we talk it out.

I hardly ever have conversations about bonuses. It turns out that most people know exactly what kind of bonus payment they deserve. I agree with almost everyone that ever asks for a higher bonus, and almost everyone who gets a lower one seems to understand.

* * *

Key Points

- Managers make it clear to everyone that we want the best for them, but that we won't act as their agents

- We tell people we will never give them a pay rise they don't ask for, but that we expect them to ask for them when they think they deserve them

- People can make a case for a pay rise whenever they want them, the manager is not responsible for regularly reviewing salary

- A default bonus payment is decided on for everyone. This payment is only higher or lower if specifically discussed

JUST GIVE THEM ACCESS TO THE KITCHEN

Personal and career development

There's one aspect of management that used to take up the vast majority of my emotional energy. It had nothing to do with our results. I never used to stress about those. I could leave work and switch off entirely no matter how things were going. Good or bad, results didn't tend to take up any of my energy once I'd left work. In fact, I was pretty much always able to compartmentalise everything, with one exception. My team's career development. When it came to that, my failures came home with me.

I think the reason for this is straightforward enough. I had a lot of selfish managers in the early stages of my career. People who didn't care one bit about me or my future, and who just took as much from me as they could get away with without ever giving anything back. When I became a manager, I was determined to never be that guy. I set myself a really simple goal that I've always stayed true to: I try to make sure that anybody who works for me is better off for having done so.

Of course, I haven't always succeeded in this goal. There are people who I have failed. But I have always tried. It has always been the single non-negotiable when it comes to how

I approach my job. And as a result, when I know I've messed that up - when I've felt like someone probably wasn't better off for having me as their manager - it hasn't been something I've been able to let go of. It has come home with me.

I explain all of this because I want the intention behind how I now approach career and personal development with Minimum Effective Management to be completely clear. Nothing about this approach is a dismissal of the needs of my staff. Those things matter to me above everything else I do in this job. However, it's undeniably true that no matter how hard your manager tries, no matter how much effort and thought they put in, they will simply never be as well placed to understand and manage your career as you are. The best thing your manager can do for you isn't manage your career - it is to give you the freedom and opportunity to manage it yourself.

A long time ago I had a friend who was part of a very wealthy family. And I mean like, British old school weird wealthy. They had a vast squadron of servants who handled pretty much everything that went on in the house. One day I was having lunch with him and his family, and his mother was complaining about the food their chef had prepared. There was nothing wrong with the food, it was incredible, but it wasn't exactly what she wanted, or prepared exactly how she wanted it. So she was annoyed. She called the chef out to tell him what was wrong, but she couldn't explain it. She knew she didn't want it the way he'd prepared it, but she couldn't really explain how she did want it. The more she struggled to explain, the more frustrated she seemed to get with him - as if he should have been able to understand her needs despite her not knowing them herself. Eventually her patience wore thin, they reached what she determined to be an understanding, and the chef walked back to the kitchen looking confused and nervous, clearly having no more idea what she wanted than she did herself.

In a nutshell, that's the problem with taking on responsibility for someone else's career. We often don't know what people want, and they often don't even know themselves. But when they expect us to be helping them progress, it becomes our fault when that progress doesn't materialise.

Finding out what someone wants from their career is a painstaking process which is difficult enough to carry out for one person, let alone several. Let's be honest, how many of us even know what we want from our own careers? It's difficult to know, and the answer is also kind of fluid. I had no idea that I wanted the career I've ended up having. The chances of us always knowing how everyone wants to progress and balancing the opportunities around our team in a fair and universally beneficial way are minuscule. If you've never had a manager who you felt wasn't giving you the opportunities you deserved, you've been a lot luckier than I have been. It happened to me constantly, and I have no doubt that I did it to people constantly too. It's simply unavoidable.

Our careers change our lives, they have a huge impact on our mental and emotional wellbeing, our ability to take care of ourselves and the people we love, and our sense of purpose and value. We're letting people down when we get this wrong. When we misunderstand their career goals, we're letting them down. When they don't get to work on the skills they want to develop, we're letting them down. I know we don't tell our staff that we take on full responsibility for their career development, but there's undoubtedly an unspoken understanding that we're going to be actively supporting them. As a result of this, they have a reasonable expectation that we will deliver on that. But we can't, not always. It's just not realistic.

Very simply, taking a hands on role in other people's career and personal development is not something we succeed at often enough. And we don't need to do it. We don't need to painstakingly find out exactly what everyone wants to eat and how they want it prepared. We don't need to slave away and try to create the perfect meal for each of them, only to find a bunch of them have allergies we didn't know about or have recently gone vegan. We can avoid all of it.

We just need to give them access to the kitchen.

With the way I now work, I make it clear to everyone that I won't take a proactive role in their career. Instead, I make sure they have an environment that allows them to grow based on their own choices. I'm available to support them however they need, but the support is reactive. They come to me, I don't drive any of it, and if someone wants to just leave me out of it entirely, they can. The result is that everyone has the opportunity to grow and develop, and nothing I may or may not do can block or hinder them.

Conveniently, when I started to think about how to deliver this, I found that I'd already laid the foundations for it when I decided not to get involved with delegating work. People were already free to choose what they worked on themselves, which meant they were already free to work on the skills they wanted to develop in order to expand or change their job role.

A crucial part of this is that there are no lines drawn

around people based on their functional job role. Everyone has freedom to work on anything they want to work on. Let's say you're a copywriter, but you would like to become a graphic designer, and you've been developing the skills required to do that in your own time. You'd now like to make that transition, or at least explore it. Consider how that would be possible in a traditional management structure. You'd have to ask your manager, who would then have to talk to the design manager. There would be headcount issues to consider, OpEx issues, discussions on training. It wouldn't be simple. If you wanted to change your career in that way, it wouldn't be something that you could just decide to pursue. Several people would have to be involved and would have to agree and would have to support you. You wouldn't have control of it.

But with the Minimum Effective Management approach, none of that is necessary. If there's a design task that needs to be completed, and you apply to work on the task and are accepted, you can do the task. You wouldn't need to have involved anyone other than the person who needed the work done. If you could convince them you could do it, then you could do it. In our company, you aren't required to solely work on tasks that are relevant to your core skill set. Over time, you might end up only doing design tasks, and then rather than me hiring the new designer we would clearly have needed if you weren't carrying out those tasks, I'll hire a new copywriter instead as you won't be doing those anymore.

One of the concerns I had about this approach related to the availability of skills. What if I hired a bunch of designers, but they all kept applying for copywriting work instead? In truth, this proved to be a complete non-issue. The vast majority of people don't carry out these drastic career transitions, and when people do it tends to be gradual. It's not an immediate switch, they just gradually pick up work they're interested in that's outside of their primary role. The safety net we have always catches any skills shortage anyway, and we're perfectly able to use our judgement to make sure silly situations don't arise. If we have a shortage of people with copywriting skills, but more than enough people with graphic design skills, and you're a copywriter who keeps applying for graphic design work, we'll just not pick you for that work. The truth is these situations, whilst hypothetically possible, just don't occur. Everyone has access to the same information as I do, so they know as well as I do if we're short on a specific skill, and they bear that in mind when making their decisions on what work to apply for. If you're a copywriter and can see a backlog of copywriting tasks, and hardly any graphic design tasks, you will handle the copywriting ones. And if you don't, that's kind of enlightening for me, in many ways.

What occurs far more often is the opposite of the thing I was concerned about. People make their choices on what work they'll apply for based on the overall situation at work. Remember, everyone has the same job description regardless of their role: *"Use your best judgement to help us achieve our goals"*. And people do exactly that. We have a number of multi-talented people in our team - people with skills that span many different functional roles. Those people often pick up tasks outside of their core skill set, not because they're trying to make a career transition, but because they could see that's how they could be the most useful at that given time. By not worrying about preventing an extremely unlikely bad outcome, we've enabled a whole host of really great outcomes and softened the walls that can form between functional roles.

Because we already worked this way, the only problem left that I needed to solve in relation to personal development was how I would allow people to learn entirely new skills. There are obviously situations where people aren't able to simply work on a skill to improve it, they actually need to learn and develop the skill in the first place.

Once again, I found that the traditional management solution to this was a result of us solving problems with control and authority, which led us to a 'swallow the fly' action. We knew people wanted training and development, so we set ourselves up as the people who would give it to them. We didn't consider just enabling them to get it for themselves. Once it was our responsibility to give them these things, that meant we had to identify and plan what that training should be and when it could take place.

I don't need to do any of that.

I give each employee a training budget, and I tell them to spend it however they choose to, on whatever training they want to do. This - coupled with their complete freedom to control their own time - is all I need to do. I'm not choosing their meals, I'm giving them access to the kitchen.

It was at around this point in the process of bui lding Minimum Effective Management that it became very clear to me how one management activity had been leading to another. This new approach was co ntinually showing me that the more problems I all owed people to solve themselves, the fewer new pr oblems I would create. Because I wasn't delegatin g, I didn't need to do as much to support career

```
development. Because I wasn't controlling people'
s time, I didn't need to arrange training. With e
ach problem I allowed to be solved with autonomy
instead of control, I seemed to prevent another p
roblem from even occurring.
```

Of course, formal training is only one aspect of personal development. A lot of development happens in a more organic way, and I wanted to make sure we had a culture where we helped each other grow. I didn't just want people to be able to take time away from work to learn whenever they wanted to, I also wanted them to be able to take time away to teach. And as it turned out, I barely needed to do anything to enable that either. It was pretty much done already. All I had to do was tell people that helping a coworker learn something was a perfectly acceptable use of their time. That was all. Working this way, our software developers have taught our designers basic CSS. Our designers have taught our developers basic design principles. I've never arranged any of it - in fact I didn't even know it happened until after the fact - everyone just arranged it themselves.

Obviously I could choose to be more restrictive with the approach. I could restrict what people can spend their training budget on, how much training they do, or what skills people can spend their time developing. The pros and cons of that are fairly obvious, and when it comes to the approach I guess it comes down to personal preference. However, my preference has been to not be restrictive at all. I believe in giving people total freedom. This means that if you're a salesperson who wants to spend the training budget I give you on a landscape gardening course that is of no benefit to the company whatsoever, you can go right ahead and do that. I want you to be better off for having worked for me, so that training budget is for you, not for me. All I need you to do is make sure you're helping us achieve our goals to the best of your ability. If you are, then you're meeting your end of the bargain. And if next year you quit to go be a gardener because it's what you've always wanted to do, and we helped you do that, I honestly can't think of a better outcome.

There's a question on this subject I've had put to me a surprising number of times. It's a push back of sorts, and I've heard it enough that I've had to accept that the solution clearly isn't as obvious as I think it should be. The question is: what do I do when I think someone needs specific training? If people control this themselves, how do I correct skill shortages I observe?

The answer is really simple. If I need someone to do some specific training...I just ask them to do the training. That's it. Nothing about this approach takes my power away. I am allowing people to make choices about what training they do, that doesn't mean I'm no longer allowed to have expectations about the skills people bring to my company. It's not an either/or situation. I'm employing you to help us achieve our goals. If you don't have the skills to do that, I'm going to ask you to develop them. It's not a big deal.

When I first made the change to work this way, a number of problems went away. One specific situation stands out in my memory. At that time, I had an employee who was really good at his job, and who wanted to progress. The problem was he really didn't know what 'progress' meant for him. He wasn't sure what he wanted to do next. I'd been trying to find opportunities for him, but nothing was a good fit. The failure to find him a new opportunity felt like mine, because I felt like he deserved it. Other people who weren't performing their jobs as well as he was but who had clearer visions of where they wanted to be were progressing beyond him, and he was starting to feel bitter about it. It had started to affect his motivation. The unspoken feeling was clearly that if I didn't appreciate him enough to promote him, he might as well stop trying. His performance started to dip significantly, and I'd all but resigned myself to the fact he was probably going to quit.

Then I reframed things with this approach. I told everyone that all of their development was entirely up to them, and that I would just guide and support them in whatever they decided to do. Suddenly, the responsibility for his career was his, not mine. And within a few days his whole attitude changed. He went back to being motivated, and he seemed to enjoy his job again. He didn't ever push for anything else. He just stayed in the role he was in and came into work smiling every day. What he realised - the moment it was actually his decision - was that he didn't really want to do anything else. Previously he'd been expecting me to solve this problem for him - like my friend's mother expecting the chef to know how she wanted her food even though she didn't know herself - and he had been getting resentful that I hadn't done it. He thought it meant I didn't value what he was doing. When I stopped trying to make his lack of direction my problem, he realised that there wasn't really a simple answer to it, and that it didn't mean I didn't appreciate him. He stopped blaming me for something that I had no control over, and just got back to enjoying a job he was good at and wanted to do.

At the same time, the people who wanted to grow were able to grow far faster than they had been with me as a gatekeeper. People were finding new opportunities in new departments, people were picking up skills entirely unrelated to the job they had but that helped them get the job they wanted. We saw people move around across all areas of the business, and this in turn meant that people who performed different functions became far more interconnected. They started to learn more about the roles one another performed, and understand the challenges one another faced. The functional based silos that traditional management fosters started to dissolve.

It hasn't just been better for the ambitious people either. I think it's also been a relief for the people who are content and enjoy their job as it is. I often think that people can feel embarrassed about being perfectly happy with the job they have, and that a lack of ambition has become something to be ashamed of. "Where do you see yourself in five years?" is a common interview question, and the implication is certainly that answering "exactly where I am now" is not an acceptable answer. But for some people, that actually is what they want. It has taken me years to realise that. As someone who has always pushed for more, I've historically projected that desire on to my staff and assumed all of them had ambitions that a lot of them probably didn't really have. Applying that pressure is actually something that we feel like we're supposed to do as managers, but I've come to realise that this pressure is unpleasant for people who are just content as things are. With the way I work now, the people who don't want to change anything never have to worry about pretending to a pushy manager that they're more ambitious than they really are. They can stay exactly where they are and nobody will ever pressure them, but if they ever decide they want to move, all the opportunities will be there for them to take.

Key Points

- People can work on whatever they want to work on to develop the skills they want to develop

- People are free to apply to work on anything they want to do, and are not restricted only to work that is relevant to their core skill set

- We give people a training budget and let them spend it however they want, and carry out the training whenever they want

- People can control when they take time away from work to learn or teach a new skill

ONE

ONE

One-on-one meetings

Although I touched on one-on-ones when I explained why I no longer have recurring meetings, I want to expand on them within the context of supporting my staff, as the one-on-one traditionally plays a large role in this.

Before I start, I should be clear that in this context I'm referring specifically to the scheduled recurring one-on-one meetings that are standard management practice, not just any one-on-one conversation that might happen as and when it's needed. If you'd asked me about these scheduled recurring one-on-ones a few years ago, I'd have told you that they were a non-negotiable. I'd have firmly stated that that they were your most important meetings, and that you should prioritise them above everything else. If you're going to approach management in the traditional way, I stand by this. Conventional management absolutely depends on the one-on-one. However, with Minimum Effective Management that is no longer necessarily the case.

The point of a one-on-one is to allow you to build a relationship with your staff so you can make sure they're getting what they need out of work. There are other benefits to them, but they're really supposed to be for the employee, not for you. They make sure your people have a chance to be heard, and they're proven to make a huge difference to employee engagement and satisfaction. However, Minimum Effective Management has taken the manager out of the equation for many of the things an employee would traditionally need to feel heard on. Their career, their salary, their work, how they spend their time, their personal development - all these things are entirely within their own hands and they can shape them without the need to involve their manager. Removing the manager as a blocker for an employee to gain a sense of autonomy, purpose, recognition and personal growth also removes the need for the manager to diligently ensure discussions around those topics are taking place.

That being said, the one-on-one is perhaps the only recurring meeting that I feel can still bring value, and it is a tool I still use. But not in the same way I used to. Today, the way I think of the one-on-one is that it's a tool I will use by default with each new employee, but with the goal of reaching the point where I no longer need it. I want to have a relationship with each of my team that means a scheduled meeting for us to talk about things isn't necessary, because we can freely communicate whenever we need to. But the fact is we probably won't have that relationship immediately. We will have to build it.

Back in my traditional management days, I found that the one-on-ones I used to have with the people I had the best relationships with never added any value. We'd walk in, sit there and try to think of something we needed to say to one another, then either walk out, or continue a conversation we'd been having earlier on anyway. When I had a good relationship with someone, we'd talked about everything already, so we didn't need a set time to get together and talk more. I kept doing them for a while - even after they were obviously pointless - because I was so stuck on the idea that they were non-negotiable. But the point of them is to give your people a chance to be heard, and if they're getting that anyway, you don't need the meetings.

To get to that stage though, we have to get to know each other. When someone first comes to work for me, we will not yet have the kind of relationship we need. They might not fully understand the level of autonomy they have, they might still be conditioned to feel they need to ask permission to do things they can actually just do, and they probably won't be fully comfortable with me right away. They're also new to the company, so are likely to have questions or concerns or will just benefit from a bit of structure while they get used to things. And we need to get to know each other. I almost feel as though people kind of need deprogramming from the old way of thinking. For example, I often have to tell new employees to stop asking my permission to take a day off at least five or six times before they just go ahead and take time off without asking me. I use the one-on-one as a way to build the trust necessary for us to no longer need the one-on-one.

Once someone is completely comfortable with me, and I know that they'll think nothing of just coming to me the moment they need something, the one-on-one will no longer serve a purpose and I stop doing it. The way I know this has happened is simple; the meetings just feel pointless when we have them. Once that's happening, I know we're where we need to be. Sometimes this happens almost immediately, sometimes it takes weeks or even months. Some people actually prefer the meetings to carry on anyway, which actually brings me to addressing a common concern: what if people actually want or need a recurring scheduled one-on-one?

I'm hoping that by now you will be able to predict the answer to this; they can just have it. I am available to all my staff as much or as little as they need me. If they want to have a regular meeting with me, we'll have one. They can have a meeting with me every day if they need one, or every week, or every month, or just randomly. My job is to help them do their job, so if they need my time, they can have it. We hopefully shouldn't need a recurring meeting, but if it's beneficial to them, then I'll do it.

Key Points

- One-on-one meetings are used by default for new employees

- The goal of the one-on-one is to help build the relationship to the point where it isn't needed anymore

- People can decide if they'd like to continue having a regular one-on-one with their manager

I BLAME
TOM HANKS

Evaluating performance

This was another difficult one for me to change my position on. My goal was to make management easier, and I knew that performance evaluation was a really time consuming and challenging part of being a manager that I'd have to re-examine. Performance reviews have a pretty shocking success rate. According to Gallup, only two in ten employees strongly agree that their performance is managed in a way that motivates them to do outstanding work[3]. And even if that wasn't the case, performance reviews clearly break one of the core Minimum Effective Management principles by placing the responsibility on the manager instead of the group. However, I used to be a huge advocate of performance reviews. I thought they were essential, and I thought the review process I used was brilliant. The idea that anything could replace it seemed fanciful to me. But a belief you won't examine is not a good thing - it's how people end up being racist or thinking they enjoy music festivals - so I stepped back from this one.

---

[3] Re-Engineering Performance Management, Gallup, https://www.gallup.com/workplace/238064/re-engineering-performance-management.aspx

Firstly, I thought about why I believed in performance reviews so much. I immediately realised it wasn't due to the results I'd had with them. It was more personal than that. I left school when I was around 14 years old. I don't think I ever really made the decision to leave, I just stopped going in. I'm not sure why I stopped going in, and I'm not sure how I got away with it. What I am sure of is that it was Tom Hanks' fault.

See, throughout the eighties, there was a seemingly endless number of movies featuring a random young guy - usually Tom Hanks - who would get a job in the mailroom of a large company, and then roughly a month later become the CEO after saying something borderline insightful in a meeting he happened to overhear whilst delivering mail. I didn't know many people with jobs while I was growing up, so as far as I was aware this was how business worked. I just needed to get a job, any job, then say something clever around the kindly owner with the nice moustache who would inevitably ask me to take over when he retired. This was my career plan.

It didn't work.

I spent roughly ten years getting fired from jobs I hated for being opinionated and difficult. Then finally, I ran into a good performance review process and a manager I actually respected. For the first time I learned what I needed to do in order to achieve the things I wanted, and my career took off. Within a few years I'd achieved more than I ever thought I would. It is in no way an exaggeration to say that at this point, I believed that having an effective performance review completely changed not just my career, but my whole life. Understandably, this influenced my view of performance reviews pretty heavily. They helped get the best out of me after all, and if they could help me, they could help anyone.

But there was something incredibly important and in hindsight incredibly obvious that I hadn't been considering: what about the ten years of failure that led up to that one success?

I had my first effective performance review in my mid-twenties. I had been working for over ten years at this point. For a decade I had been at work, wanting to do well, wanting to progress and to learn and to thrive. And I'd been getting nowhere. I'd been disruptive to my company and coworkers, and I'd been frustrated, angry and ineffectual. And I was having performance reviews throughout that time. Every year I had one. If performance reviews were meant to improve performance, why hadn't they improved mine? They failed consistently for ten years, and then when one finally did what it was supposed to do, I viewed the entire exercise as a success. I ignored all the failures, decided performance reviews were great, then simply stopped examining that belief.

Once I realised that my faith in performance reviews wasn't really evidence based, I stopped to consider what they'd really achieved for me over all the years I'd religiously practised them. Immediately, I realised something that also should have always been obvious to me - they hadn't been that effective. I'd been performing them with this picture in my mind of the one perfect review, focussing on the big wins when I delivered it. I'd been ignoring the many times I'd crashed. In reality, those big wins weren't that common, and objectively there had not been a great deal of tangible benefit to a lot of the reviews I'd delivered.

With my brain actually engaged with the reality of the situation, I realised why I'd finally had that good performance review all those years ago. It wasn't the review. It was the manager who delivered it. He was exceptional. Not just good - exceptional. He is probably to this day the best manager I've ever known. That's how good he needed to be to make the performance review work. Not only that, I realised that the performance review hadn't even worked the way I thought it had anyway. Up until then, I'd thought that I'd improved my behaviour as a result of the performance review. That wasn't what happened. My behaviour had stayed almost exactly the same. The reason the review had worked is that the manager used it to set me expectations that actually played to my skills and natural traits, then reviewed me on those strengths instead of my weaknesses. He knew I was comfortable calling out things that I didn't think were right, but that I could also be disruptive when things were going to plan. So he put me in situations where stuff was going wrong anyway and let me shake things up. The review itself didn't do anything, I'd just had a great manager who knew how to take advantage of my strengths, rather than try to work on my weaknesses. The thing that made a difference to me wasn't the performance review. That was just the tool a great manager used to get the best out of me. The manager was the important variable, not the review. I'm sure that with any other tool, he'd have achieved the same result.

With all of this being the case, I realised that performance reviews couldn't have a place in Minimum Effective Management. If performance reviews were a flying manoeuvre, they would be the one in that Denzel Washington movie where he lands the plane upside down whilst drunk.

Possible to get right from time to time? Maybe. But not the default way anyone should try to do it.

Having dismantled my resistance to letting go of this responsibility, I now just had to work out an easier way to achieve what performance reviews are supposed to achieve. As it turns out, performance reviews are one of those tools we often try to use for several purposes. For example, the review process I used would set expectations, measure and help improve performance, and inform managers regarding reward. The immediate good news for me was that Minimum Effective Management had already taken care of setting expectations and informing reward. With the way I was going to work, the same things were expected of everyone, so there would be no need to set expectations on an individual basis. Also, people were going to be making their own case for improved reward, so it wouldn't be necessary for me to establish a process for determining that either.

This meant that all I needed to find was a way to measure and help improve individual performance.

When I examined that requirement and how performance reviews had been meeting it, it was immediately obvious to me that they were another boiling frog solution. Performance reviews may have once been the best way to meet this requirement, but they certainly aren't anymore. Technology has changed since the performance review was conceived. Back then, a manager would have been necessary to collect and deliver the information that was shared in the performance review. They would have needed to speak to other people in the company to get feedback, they would have needed to have observed the individual over the review period and measured the outcomes, and they would have needed to share that information with the people being reviewed. All of that has changed. It's no longer necessary to rely on one person to be responsible for an evaluation. And that's great, because having one person do this is inherently flawed.

When a manager is responsible for your evaluation, your actual performance is not going to be the only thing that determines the result. I have performed countless performance reviews. I have always tried to be fair, I have always tried to be objective. But I am a human being and I am therefore prone to human behaviours, and there is no way the outcomes of those reviews hasn't been shaped by my relationship with the people in question. There's a perception error sometimes known as halo and horns, which means that once we decide someone is bad, we tend to see the bad in most of the things they do, and once we decide they're good, we tend to see the good. See Donald Trump and Barack Obama - no matter which side of that someone is on, you can be reasonably sure that they believe their guy has almost never done anything wrong, and the other guy is one of history's greatest monsters. Very few people are immune to this behaviour - and certainly not the one in seven people who perform management duties. I doubt there is a manager in history who has a perfect track record of delivering completely fair performance evaluations.

I have had managers who didn't like me and who I could do no good for, and I've had others who thought I was great and who were completely happy to overlook the many unprofessional behaviours I am prone to exhibiting. As an employee, I have pretty much exclusively been viewed as either the star pupil, or the problem child. In fact, I've never had a manager who didn't either fire me or promote me within a year. But as I mentioned a moment ago, my behaviour has pretty much always been the same. The exact same behaviours that saw me get fired from every job I had up until my mid-twenties also saw me get given opportunities, get promoted and ultimately become successful. My behaviour wasn't really changing, but the person evaluating me was.

Apart from the unavoidable inconsistency of having one individual evaluate another, there's another really obvious flaw with it. Those managers - the people evaluating us - they are very rarely the people we actually work directly with. Most of us spend the vast majority of our time working with people other than our manager. It's really the views of those people that can paint the clearest picture of our performance and how it has impacted the company as a whole. If we're evaluated by the people we work with instead of our managers, it's going to be a far more realistic reflection of how we've actually performed.

This isn't a new observation of course. 360 Degree Feedback was an attempt to address this. However, I am yet to see an implementation of this that I consider even remotely useful. Due to the time it takes to give and evaluate the feedback, it's typically done with samples. It's not feedback from everyone you've worked with, it's from a sample of people you've worked with, and the samples are only collected periodically. This suffers from the same flaws as having a manager be responsible for your evaluation. There's a randomness to what that evaluation will say. With a small sample size, it's inevitable that some people are going to get lucky and only get evaluations from the people that appreciate their qualities, and some people who will experience the exact opposite. Not only that, but the evaluation itself is still almost always delivered through your manager, so their opinion can and most likely will have a disproportionate influence on the result.

I've often heard this margin of error described as acceptable. I disagree with that entirely. I understand that in purely mathematical terms, it may be an acceptable margin of error, and if we were working with drones that would be fine, but they're human beings. When you work for an entire year, and your professional future is directly affected by the results of a review, that review must be fair. It simply must be. We cannot subject people to a system and say, "hey, sometimes it's unfair, but most of the time it's not so it doesn't matter". If you're the person it's unfair to, the fact it's usually fair is of no comfort at all. As managers, we need to care about this for reasons other than the obvious moral ones. From a purely pragmatic standpoint, our lives are made so much harder when we give someone a review they feel is unfair. People who get unfair reviews require a huge amount of management. It's often the first event in a chain that leads to someone becoming incredibly difficult to manage.

I know what you're thinking. You're thinking, "Matt, you idiot, why didn't you look at 1980s professional tennis for the answer!?". Well, just calm yourself down. That's exactly what I did.

Back in the eighties, tennis used to include wave after wave of adults having full blown tantrums. It was like Twitter, but real. The line judges would call something in or out, and the player would be convinced that it was the wrong decision. He was usually the person closest to the ball when it landed so he was in the best position to see if it actually was in or out, which only made the injustice even harder to accept. The result was usually him totally losing his mind. He would scream and shout and smash rackets. Some players would become convinced that the umpire and line judges were out to get them. It would get epic.

This was tennis. No amount of fines or incentives or talks with the players seemed to change anything. Throughout my early life, tantrums of an epic scale were part of tennis. Then in 2006, they introduced Hawkeye, a system that tracked exactly where the ball actually landed. Now, when the umpire or a line judge made a call, and the player disagreed, the player could challenge it. Then they'd watch Hawkeye show where the ball landed, and correct the decision if they needed to. Tantrums pretty much entirely disappeared.

Here's the interesting thing about this. Hawkeye wasn't infallible, and everyone knew that. It might be now, but back then it would still make mistakes. But nobody seemed to mind. The vast majority of the time, players still accepted the decision it made without anger or frustration. The reason for this was that they knew it was at least consistent and without an agenda. Everyone was being judged to the same standard by the same technology. There was no sense of injustice anymore. Hawkeye couldn't be shaped by personal bias, it couldn't be out to get anyone. It could make mistakes, but they were just mistakes. And people could accept that.

To make management easier when it came to evaluating performance, I decided I needed a Hawkeye. I needed a way to show people in a consistent and unchallengeable way, "this is how you've performed", and have them know that my individual view of them couldn't possibly have played a part in that evaluation. And that problem, in its most basic form, had already been solved.

Think about how Uber gathers feedback on drivers and riders. They don't have a manager who evaluates each driver, and they don't poll a select group of drivers and riders every few months to ask how everyone is performing. At the end of each journey, the driver rates the rider, and the rider rates the driver. These ratings make up an overall score, and that score tells everyone how well they're performing their part in the exchange.

Now, you might dismiss this. It's only Uber, after all. But before you do that, it's worth considering that every single driver will attest to the fact that the moment Uber came along with that rating, the way people behaved in their cars improved immeasurably. Using that score - that incredibly simple score - Uber was able to improve the behaviour of millions of drunk people they'd never met, all over the world, without ever having a conversation with them or even setting an expectation of them. It reduced violence, abuse, general rudeness, and damage to the vehicles.

Can you imagine trying to achieve the same thing with a performance review?

You might also think that the score out of 5 is too simplistic. If you do, I'm 100% with you on that. But again, on closer consideration you'll see that the Uber score is almost certainly far more informative than the scores we use for performance reviews. Those scores are also typically out of 5. But with Uber, unlike with the performance review, at least the rating is a genuine reflection of how people have perceived your performance and not a pretty much arbitrary decision made by one individual.

The performance review score has long been something that bothered me, even before Minimum Effective Management. My biggest issue with it is that it is not actually a true reflection of your performance - it's relational to the people in your team. Most companies have unspoken quotas for how many people can get top performance scores on each team. They might not outright tell you there's a limit, but if you tried to give everyone in your team a top rating, you wouldn't be allowed to. I even worked for a company once where an HR investigation was triggered if someone was given a maximum performance score. Think about how stupid these two directives are for a moment. Your job as a manager is to ensure your people perform to the highest standard possible, yet you are told that only some of your people actually should, and if you claim one of them actually did, they'll assume it's a lie. This is the opposite of what we should be encouraging. A high performing team would see everyone perform to the highest standard. They would respect, value and support one another, and as a team they would produce great results. Together. But if I'm in a team where I can only achieve a top performance rating - which will likely play a factor in determining my reward - if my colleagues don't do the same, I am being actively incentivised not to support them. It turns my coworkers into competitors.

This isn't just bad for the people getting the scores, it's also bad for the company. Imagine you're the manager of a team that's performing terribly. Every member of every other team works much much harder and gets much better results than all the people on your team. But how would you know that? You only have a view of your own team. Not only that, it's your job to make them perform well, so if you were to record scores that said everyone that worked for you was terrible, you'd actually be saying that you had done a terrible job yourself. So, when the time to review people comes along, you're not going to do that. What you're going to do is assign your performance scores relational to the people on your team. Your top performer - who in the context of the entire company is still a terrible performer - is very likely to be given a high performance score, simply by being the best of a bad bunch. Meanwhile, someone who has performed far better on a different team where everyone excelled will be given a lower score, just because they were unlucky enough to have worked on a team of exceptional performers.

The scoring system, when performance reviews are handled by a manager, creates false silos and irrational performance comparisons that result in the company evaluating performance unfairly, and assigning reward and opportunity to the wrong people.

Everyone knows it's nonsense as well. In literally every single company I have ever worked, the performance review scoring process has been openly mocked the moment nobody important was around. It's an unfair and mostly meaningless score that people don't take seriously at all, and if it wasn't for the fact it determined their reward they wouldn't care about it in the slightest.

Compare that to the way people see their Uber rating. If you have any doubt as to how seriously people take that, I suggest you log on to a dating app and see how long it takes you to find someone who has put their Uber rating on their bio. People actually take pride in that score - albeit ironically – even though it's just a rating of how well they've behaved in a taxi. The reason they take it seriously is that it's a true reflection of reality. It's not fake. It's not the subjective opinion of one person. Every driver they've ever interacted with has contributed to that score, so it is fair and accurate. That's all people need.

I have never once seen someone put their latest performance review score on their dating bio.

However, the five star rating system Uber uses is a little bit too Orwellian for the kind of workplace I wanted to create. The main problem is what I call the *default five* problem. If you use Uber, you'll know that the etiquette is roughly as follows:

- If you're a rider, and you don't vomit over the seats or abuse the driver - you expect to get a five star rating

- If you're a driver, and you don't steal from or kidnap the rider - you expect to get a five star rating

Everyone starts at five, and works their way down. This means by default, we expect to be rated as the absolute best, and we're annoyed at anything less than that. When someone gives us a rating below five stars, we feel like they're telling us that we're terrible people. This leaves us no room to be acknowledged for being exceptional. If the hypothetical Genie I mentioned earlier got into an Uber and started dishing out wishes, the driver wouldn't be able to give that Genie a rating any higher than the one he gave the previous rider who simply hadn't verbally abused him.

So, in short, I wanted the Uber system - but not quite.

The approach I wanted to find was one that leveraged all the power of the Uber rating and that was as convenient and easy to maintain, but that didn't have a *default five* problem. I also wanted it to give people information they could actually use to help them improve specific areas of their performance, not just a generic overall score.

Ongoing work centric feedback

I decided do this by gathering feedback from everyone who had been involved in a project, whenever that project was completed. This would be very similar to the way Uber ask for feedback at the end of every journey. Whenever a project is completed, everyone involved in that project is asked these three questions about one another:

- Did they have the skills they said they had?
  (No/Yes/They could do more)

- Did they do everything they said they'd do?
  (No/Yes/They did even more)

- Would you be happy to work with them again?
  (No/Yes/Delighted)

Notice that the middle answer to each question is perfectly acceptable. It's also the default answer. Giving this answer doesn't seem as negative as giving someone a three out of five star rating, even though it's mathematically slightly worse.

In practise, this middle answer is almost always the one we each give one another. Most of us just do a perfectly acceptable job. But every now and then, one of us is awesome, and someone else recognises that. We can also leave comments, but it isn't required, and to be honest we hardly ever do. I haven't found that they're needed very often.

Let me take a moment to explain why I ask those three specific questions. Whenever I'm considering hiring someone, I always consider these three things:

- Can they do the job?

- Will they do the job?

- Do I want them to do the job?

I do this because when you just evaluate someone as a whole, if they're exceptional in one of those areas it can blind you to the fact that they're really lacking in another. Before I thought about things this way, I occasionally hired people I shouldn't have hired, on the basis they were clearly exceptionally capable. This fact had then blinded me to some red flags about how they would actually apply that capability. Someone might have all the skills they need to do a job, but also be unreliable or lazy. They might not actually do the job, even if they are perfectly capable of it. Equally, you might find someone that can and will do the job, but who will be intractable or simply unpleasant to deal with, and you'd just sooner someone else did it. Those are the three areas that will really determine if someone is going to be successful in a role or not.

I worked with a software engineer a little while back, before I used Minimum Effective Management. Everyone agreed he was one of our best software engineers. That wasn't in question. He had ambition to take a leading role on our software team, and there was an opening for that to happen. He was a really smart guy, and he was more than capable of doing the job. He also worked really hard, was really dependable, and had great ideas. He both could and would have done the job. But he was a nightmare to work with. He just didn't listen, he thought he was smarter than everyone else, and I just didn't believe he'd be a positive force in the leadership team at the time. Despite his talent, it just didn't make sense to give him the role.

When I told him I was choosing someone else, I gave him my honest reasons. He didn't take it very well. As far as he was concerned it was completely unfair and the view I was expressing about him was totally unrelated to his job. He considered it to be personal. In a sense, he was right. It was personal in as much as I felt his personality would cause problems for the rest of the team. It wasn't personal in the sense that I didn't like him though - I actually liked him quite a lot - but to him, none of that mattered. I remember thinking at the time that if he'd been able to see that everyone we worked with pretty much felt the same way, he'd have been far more likely to take it onboard. If he'd done that, he'd actually have been able to work on the thing that was getting in his way. Instead, he was undoubtedly going to walk away and carry on focussing on how capable he was, assuming that I just had a personal problem with him. He wouldn't fix the problem. He handed his notice in a few days later, and we went on to function much better as a team despite losing one of our strongest people.

A couple of weeks later I happened to meet up with an old boss of mine. He was someone I had a lot of respect for, but at the same time I had always been aware that he didn't particularly like me all that much. Not in a bad way, I just always knew that we weren't really on the same wavelength. I talked to him about the frustration of not being able to help this guy see that this behaviour was getting in his own way. As I was explaining it to him, he started laughing, then said "that's exactly how I felt about you, Matt".

Shit.

I knew he was totally right. Throughout most of my career I'd been slamming how right I thought I was down everyone's throat, and I did it so often that eventually a lot of people stopped caring what I had to say even when they agreed with me. They just decided that the room would be an easier place to be in if I wasn't in it, even if I was right. My reaction to this was always, "I can't believe these idiots can't see how right I am!" and I'd just double down on the same behaviour and become even harder to work with.

If I'd ever worked in a company that had asked everyone I worked with the three questions I ask people now, I'm convinced I would have seen an undeniable trend. Instead of being outraged that people couldn't see how right I was, I'd realise that nobody was questioning my ability. Nobody was saying that I couldn't do the job. All they were saying was that they didn't want me to do it because I made their job harder or less pleasant. They'd have said they didn't want to work with me, even though they knew I was good at what I did. That would have been really useful for me to know. It would have saved me a lot of wasted time doing the opposite of what I actually needed to do.

Years of performance reviews, and I never learned that about myself. Never even got close. I had definitely been told, but I had always written it off as a personal issue, just like my problem employee had done. I couldn't have done that if the view had been expressed by the majority of people I'd worked with. The information I gather for people now lets them really compartmentalise how the way they perform impacts the people they work with, and it doesn't allow them to dismiss what they're told as just the personal bias of one manager or one individual. Of course, someone you work with might have a personal problem with you and give you unfair feedback. But we ask everyone you work with, so the only way that eventuality could go on to have a serious effect on your overall result is if everyone has a personal problem with you. And if everyone has a personal problem with you, I'm afraid the chances are that you might actually be the problem.

The best way to collect this information is obviously to follow the Uber example and use technology. We use an internal tool which allows me to be fairly detached from the whole process. I pay attention to what's going on, and keep an eye out for dips in performance so I can get involved if I think I need to, but I very rarely have to. People get their feedback, and they take it seriously. It matters to them. I've made sure we've avoided creating a creepy Orwellian culture by not structuring the questions in a way that creates a *default five* problem, and by not assigning an overall score to people. The feedback we get really just acts as a guide rail so we each know how the people we work with perceive us, and can identify when we need to make changes.

Working this way isn't just fairer, it also brings social incentives to the forefront of how we get things done. As I mentioned before, the recognition most people really crave is from their peers, not from their manager. This system gives people genuine recognition for their contributions - good or bad. When we perform well in a certain area, other people let us know, and we try to keep that going. When we perform badly and people let us know, we usually seek to address it without the need for anyone to prompt us. Almost always, if someone isn't getting good feedback, they will seek to address that themselves, and ask for the support they need.

I honestly believe that the answers to those three questions are the only feedback any employee ever needs in order to work on improving their performance. No matter what you're doing or how you work, those questions are going to be relevant when it comes to how people interoperate. How an individual would go about addressing it when the answers aren't positive will be different for all of us, but the value of the questions themselves is universal. Working this way gives me and everyone that works with me genuinely valuable feedback that fairly measures their performance, and that can't be unfairly influenced by any one individual's view.

Key Points

- We decentralise performance evaluation by gathering feedback from everyone

- There is no performance review, just an ongoing process of gathering information about how we each perform

- We collect feedback that will enable people to see specifically which area of their performance they might need to improve

- We support people who don't get great feedback, and we leave everyone else to get on with it

I
HATED
HIS
FACE

Management relationships

I've kept this to the end because it's not going to be an option for everyone. All the other aspects of Minimum Effective Management can be adopted to some degree by managers at any level, but in order for this to be something you can implement, you would need to have a very broad reach across your company and be able to change the management function as a whole. If you don't have that kind of influence, don't worry. This isn't essential. Everything else still works perfectly well even if you can't make this change, but I think the benefits of adopting this way of working are huge.

I don't have functional managers anymore. In fact, I don't define functional departments at all, not in an operational sense. This thinking has already started to find its way into a lot of organisations. Cross-functional teams are becoming more prevalent. However, I've noticed that when these cross-functional teams are implemented, they are often just overlaid across an existing functional hierarchy, which kind of defeats the purpose and limits their benefit. The way most organisations adopt cross-functional teams is to retain the functional departments, but have members of those departments move around various cross-functional teams as well, often getting themselves two bosses in the process. So, the design team will still have a design manager, and the designers will still report to the design manager, but those designers will also be part of cross-functional teams and those cross-functional teams will also have a leader. Rather than simplifying things, this actually complicates them.

I don't do this. I think this gets us the worst of both worlds, not the best.

One of the main reasons I don't have functional managers is that I believe management is a vocation in its own right. Management is an entirely separate skill from the other functions we hire for. I don't believe there should be such a thing as a design manager or a software development manager. There should just be a manager. And that manager should be picked solely on their ability to manage people. When we select functional managers, we typically require the manager to also have the skills that function requires. This broadens the skills a manager needs even further, to the point that it becomes extraordinarily unlikely that we'll find a good candidate. Having all the skills needed to be a great manager is hard enough, if you also need to be great at your specific function, it's becoming ridiculous. Demanding that the leader of your software development team must be a great software developer and be a great manager is like refusing to let someone play the piano unless they're also a great wrestler. They are entirely different skills. Picking people on that basis isn't going to get you the best piano player or the best wrestler. At best it will probably only get you someone average at both. On top of this, when we pick functional managers, their skill in their specific function usually takes far greater precedence than their skill as a manager, so we saddle people with managers who aren't up to the task of managing, and who therefore need to rely on their functional skills to make things happen. This will of course mean that their staff are given less autonomy as the manager has no option but to micromanage them.

It's not necessary to do this. A good manager can manage anyone, regardless of their own functional skills. The point of management is that you use the skills of other people to make a thing happen. I have proven to be pretty good at managing software developers, despite being a truly horrible software developer myself and still kind of believing that computers might actually be made of magic. The vast majority of the people I manage have skills I don't possess or often even understand. Good management does not require function specific knowledge, I sometimes think it's actually easier without it. It's hard to micromanage someone if you haven't got the first clue how they do their job.

The way I work today, functional teams still exist and still have voices that get heard, but these teams aren't operational units. They're not on the org chart, and there are no functional managers. Our managers are people who are good at managing people, and any given manager might be managing people spanning several different functional roles. We base the employee-manager relationship around personality fit, not functional fit.

Working this way gives us a level of freedom that prevents so many traditional management problems ever arising. Most of us have experienced having a manager that just didn't feel like the right manager for us, and most managers have experienced managing someone that we just didn't feel like we could get through to. The problem with the functional manager structure is that your manager is determined by your shared function, not your human relationships. If the person who manages your function isn't a good fit for you on a human level, you're stuck with them. And when we give someone a manager they don't have a good relationship with, we get nothing but problems.

When we assign people a manager based solely on function, I think we're really ignoring the importance of that relationship, and treating it as a box ticking exercise. Sure, when we do it this way we can always look at an org chart and follow lines up from boxes and say to ourselves, "Yep, every box has a box above it - so everyone has a manager who supports them". That might feel comforting, but in the real world we haven't achieved anything. That's only a chart. It's not true unless the people make it true in the real world, and if they don't connect on a personal level, that relationship will bring no benefit to anyone.

Moving boxes around on an org chart cannot create these relationships. Most of the managers that have been assigned to me have been a million miles away from inspirational. I once worked for a man who remains comfortably the stupidest person I've ever met. When I first joined the company, I reported to someone I had a good relationship with. But she left not long after I joined and was replaced with someone I had absolutely no respect for. Every decision he made was cowardly and ill-informed, and he'd lie to me constantly. He'd tell me he was going to do one thing before doing the opposite, and then he'd pretend we'd never had the initial conversation. He was everything I felt a person shouldn't be, let alone a leader. Also - and maybe this shouldn't have been important to me but it absolutely was - I hated his face. He had a really creepy vibe about him. He had the kind of face you'd expect to see as the hood got pulled off your head in a horror movie torture basement. For all I know all that other horrible stuff I just said about him might not even be true. I might have just not liked him.

Either way, I was not inspired, and I didn't want him as my manager.

But my functional department gave me that clown, and I had no say in it. In fact, nobody had any say in it. There was simply no way it could change. I'd have regular meetings with him, and every now and then he'd try to say something inspirational and encouraging, and it was awful. It was such an awkward experience, because we both knew I hated him with the power of a thousand suns. He was so clearly uncomfortable even trying to manage me - it was like having a sex talk with an emotionally repressed dad. I would barely be listening to him and would just be thinking to myself, "This is not the relationship we have. Just leave it".

But after becoming a manager myself, I looked back and I felt sorry for that guy. Once I experienced being on his side of the table, I realised he was in a horrible situation too. Some time ago, I inherited a team to manage, one of whom absolutely hated me. She hated me from the get go, and I was never going to be able to turn it around. I knew it, she knew it, and we both knew the other knew it. I was as far away from inspirational to her as anyone could be. Our weekly meetings were torture for me and I'm sure even worse for her. But I had no option but to carry on the charade. I couldn't just give up and say, "Nope, not managing this one. She hates me". I had to keep trying to inspire her to perform, she had to keep pretending not to hate me, and nothing good came of any conversation we ever had. I am convinced she was worse at her job as a result of reporting to me, and this one bad relationship sucked away so much of my energy that I was worse at mine too. It was terrible for both of us. The relationship finally ended when she quit. Just like the relationship I had with my uninspiring boss ended when I quit. What else can really happen? I know I had the potential to be a good employee when I quit that job, and I know she had the potential to be good when she quit hers. But functional management forced relationships on us that couldn't possibly have created a good outcome, and gave us no escape other than quitting. Moving away from the anecdotal for a moment and into the world of data, a poll of one million US employees conducted by Gallup found that 75% of people who quit their roles do so because of their boss, not the role itself[4]. This is an expensive problem.

And it's a problem that is avoidable. In the example of my employee, I happen to know there was another manager in the business who she had a great deal of respect for. The two of them just clicked. She would have been far better off if he was her manager, but as he managed a completely different function, that was never on the table. Our functional structure stopped us solving the problem.

That's part of the reason I work completely differently. Our managers operate independently of function, and our staff can move to different managers if a specific relationship isn't working out for them. That never has to be a reflection of either the manager or the employee. Sometimes a relationship just doesn't work, and we allow people to move

---

[4] State of the American Workplace, Gallup,
https://www.gallup.com/workplace/238085/state-american-workplace-report-2017.aspx

around if that's the case. Managers don't need functional knowledge because we allow people to make their own decisions about their work, so any manager can manage any employee, regardless of their skill set. What managers need to be able to do is coach effectively, listen, help people make rational decisions, and give people support when they need it. We need to care about people, want the best for them, want to help them, and want to see them and the company succeed. We don't need to understand their job, we need to understand them. And that is function agnostic.

As I mentioned earlier, we do still have functional teams. Initially I disbanded them entirely, but they naturally reformed on their own. It turned out people naturally gravitated to other people who faced the same challenges as them, and who they could discuss their specific skills with. So functional teams have emerged more as a social part of our business than an operational one. Slack channels got created, get-togethers were arranged, that kind of thing. There are also still strong voices that represent each function. If someone feels a particular function as a whole is suffering or could benefit as a result of something changing, these strong voices speak up. We haven't lost anything by removing functional departments and managers, we've just decentralised the things they used to do.

Key Points

- Managers are chosen based on their ability to manage and not based on their functional skills

- The manager - employee relationships are determined based on personality fit, rather than skill or functional fit

- Functional teams are no longer organisational units, but they have formed organically so people with similar skills can share ideas

Providing what they need - Recap

- **People are responsible for their own salary** - Salary is not connected to recognition. There is no annual pay review and every employee is told that they will never be offered a pay rise, but they are expected to negotiate for them

- **People are free to pursue their career choices** - Managers are no longer gatekeepers of how people progress their careers. People can apply to work on any task they are capable of completing, regardless of their primary skill set

- **One-on-one meetings are optional** - When an employee starts working with a new manager, the one-on-one is used as a way of building the relationship. The goal is to reach a point that it is no longer needed

- **Performance evaluation is decentralised** - Performance is no longer reviewed by managers on a periodic basis. Instead it's an ongoing process where each individual provides feedback on the colleagues

- **Managers are chosen based on their management ability** - We have no functional departments and no functional managers. All manager-employee relationships are based on personality fit, not functional fit. Employees can change managers if a relationship isn't working

6

PUTTING IT ALL TOGETHER

Managers have always been fans of buzzwords. Proactive is probably the king of them all. We love to be proactive. Whatever occurs, we want to have known about it beforehand. We all want to be prescient soothsayers who are constantly ahead of the game. We expect to know in advance what each day will bring and we plan accordingly.

Well, that's nothing like my working day.

A typical day for me involves responding to events that my safety nets have caught, so I almost always start work with a completely clear calendar, and no real idea what I'll be doing, or who I'll be talking to. Then I find out what the day needs from me.

My first task of the day is to share the information I need to share to ensure the safety nets all work correctly. This might be an update on a goal I'm the representative for, an estimate on when I'll finish some work, or feedback on people I've been working with on a project. Whatever it is, the start of the day is dedicated to making sure I've shared all the information I need to share. This is the same for everyone else in the business.

Once I've done this - which usually only takes a few minutes - I then take a look at what our various safety nets have caught. I tend to start with the tasks my staff are working on. I check their estimate trends and see if anyone is drifting off track, and if it looks like I might need to talk to someone, I ping them a message to ask if they're free. This is usually my priority - keeping the work flowing. It's not unusual for me to be unaware of what someone is working on before I talk to them. If it's the first time I've needed a conversation with them about that piece of work, all I'll know about it is how the estimate trend has progressed up until that point. This doesn't matter at all. What I'm finding out is why the work isn't on track, and what needs to happen to get it back on track. The most helpful things a manager can provide are very rarely specific to the work. They are far more often about helping people organise their thoughts or about bringing people together. Through basic coaching we can work out what needs to be done and who needs to do it, even if I don't really understand what they're actually working on.

Once I know my team are all able to keep working without any blockers, I'm free to concentrate on other things. Next up I'll take a look at the latest updates from each of the goal representatives. I'll see how each goal is progressing, and consider if we're focusing our attention on the right things. If I have questions, I might chat to the other Decision Makers over Slack, or we might even get together if there are a bunch of things to discuss.

When I'm happy that we're still focusing on the right things, and that all my staff are working unhindered, I take a look at the latest feedback. This usually takes just a few minutes. I look for people who are getting great feedback, and people who are getting bad feedback. If I see anything that I think might suggest a conversation would be a good idea, then I'll give the people in question a shout.

Typically within no more than a couple of hours each day I know that the essential part of my job is done, and that if I stopped working at that point, everything would still be ok. Sometimes that's exactly what I do. Most of the time though, I take advantage of the most valuable thing a leader can have - time to think. With no real pressure to do anything essential, I can get my head into whatever I want. Sometimes I take a look at our skills coverage to make sure we're going to be able to deliver the upcoming tasks we have planned. That helps me stay ahead of any problems and informs me regarding hiring decisions. Sometimes I just think about the business or the industry as a whole, where things are heading, what we're doing, the problems we solve today and the problems we might solve in the future. Sometimes I write a book, which is how we ended up here.

Whatever I do with that time, I know that the core part of my job is handled, and I can give the thing I'm doing my full attention without getting pulled into anything that doesn't really matter to me. I'm not going to be pulled away just to go and sit in a meeting that I'm not going to contribute much to. I'm not going to have to prepare a bunch of reports and presentations for people who are going to all but ignore them, and who don't really need to know what I'd be telling them anyway. I'm just going to work on something I want to work on that I think might help us achieve the goals we're all trying to achieve.

Sometimes I'm called on to do something else. Someone might want some advice, or just to talk to me about their work in general. One of my team might have prepared a case for getting a pay rise, so I might have a conversation with them about that. I'm almost always available, because my time hasn't been booked up in advance. Bear in mind that as we have no functional departments, there is never any need for departmental heads to get together either - departmental heads don't even exist. We have a team of Decision Makers, and sometimes we get together to discuss what work we'll pick up next, but other than that there is no operational need for meetings of any kind, so it's incredibly rare for me to be unavailable when someone genuinely needs to talk to me.

However my day turns out, I always feel in control, I always feel completely informed, and I always feel like I'm using my time in the best way I could be using it.

7

TAKING THE PLUNGE

Although my fellow managers have yet to have me committed to an asylum, when I have shared these ideas I have often found myself met with the appeal to a common practice. What I've noticed is that even when people have agreed with and understood everything I've said about how and why this approach works for me, they have still seemed reluctant to implement the changes themselves. It's just not how management is done, after all. Sometimes I think it's as though we've had the stabilisers on our bike for so long that the idea of taking them off seems terrifying to us. I've always hoped to find a magic bullet response to this objection. A way of alleviating the understandable fear of trying something completely different. I haven't found it. The best I can do is this:

What do you have to lose?

Unless traditional management is going so well for you that you're getting all the results you need and all your people are fully engaged and happy, then what harm could trying something else really do? There's nothing to stop you going back to the way things were if it doesn't work out. Nothing has to be set in stone. If you don't already have a perfectly efficient workplace with super engaged people, you potentially have an incredible amount to gain from trying even a small part of this approach, and almost nothing to lose.

I have seen first-hand that the things people have been screaming out for at work - autonomy, purpose, growth and recognition - are easily delivered if we get out of their way. My staff get to shape what their days look like, and decide what goals they'll contribute to and how they'll go about doing that. They're connected to the real purpose behind all those choices and in fact they *have* to understand that purpose in order to make the choices to begin with.

They get true recognition, not just from me, but from everyone they work with. And there's a responsibility that comes with that. They aren't just praised for doing a good job while I sweep their failures under the carpet. They experience true recognition - the good and the bad. They are connected to the real consequences of their actions, and that gives those actions meaning. This environment lets them truly grow. They work on the skills they want to develop. They see how their behaviour impacts others. They share the failures and the successes that I experience.

And the whole time, I'm really not doing that much. I let people be responsible for themselves and as a result they step up and act responsibly. On the rare occasions they don't, I'm able to give those situations my full attention and handle them in whatever way is necessary.

I know that more than ever, we're afraid of making

mistakes. We are worried that if we do something and it turns out to be the wrong choice, we'll walk right into failure. So we're cautious and we control and we try to stay on top of every decision - and the failure we were so scared of just comes right up behind us. I've found that failure is very rarely at the end of any path I choose to take, as long as I keep going. Failure is not in front of us, it's behind us. It's chasing us. If we take any path and we just keep going, it usually won't catch up. But if we stand still or if we drag our feet, it most certainly will. If we let our people help us, if we truly let them off the leash that management has put on them and we allow them to use the full power of their judgement to get us where we want to go, work becomes a far more rewarding place for everyone, and success will come along with that.

There are a bunch of ways you can be a better manager. You can get great at feedback, coaching, and communicating. You can learn what each of your people need and you can do everything in your power to make those things happen for them. You can analyse and plan and strategise until your brain hurts and your eyes bleed. And if you're lucky, you will sometimes get it all right. Once or twice I've even managed to get it right myself. Being great at management is possible, but it's exhausting.

But being a great manager doesn't have to be. Not if we change what a manager is supposed to be. It's time to reverse the trend of expecting more and more of ourselves as managers. We need to bring our people into the problems, and empower them to find their own solutions. We have to stop thinking we are responsible for them. They can do more for us. They want to do more for us.

Our job as a manager is to generate the best results with

the people we have available, and we should be finding the path of least resistance to do that. Increasingly, that is becoming less management centric. It's achieved by trusting our people to make choices. This can't be a fake trust where we give them the impression of autonomy but still seek to control everything they do. It has to be a real and genuine trust. We have to treat them as equals, not to trick them into feeling better about themselves, but because they actually are equals. We have to trust them to make good decisions, and believe that they are just as capable of doing so as we are. We have to give them access to all the information they need to make those decisions well. We have to step back. We have to let people thrive.

I'm going to close with a story. If you ignore everything else you've read in this book, you can probably get away with it if you don't ignore the thing I learned from this exchange. Looking back over my career, I'm fairly sure this one simple thing allowed me to become a successful manager despite being consistently terrible at all the things a manager is supposed to be good at.

Many years ago now, I was at a rapidly growing company with a lot of other inexperienced managers. We were all given management training as a group each week, and after the sessions we'd go off to our respective departments to try to implement the things we had been taught.

At the end of our first year together, an employee satisfaction survey was carried out, and as part of our training we all got together to go through the results for our respective departments. We found a clear difference between how the employees in my department answered compared to how everyone else did. Overwhelmingly, people in my department said they felt valued, that they believed I had their best interests at heart, and that they felt that I cared about their well-being. This was not the same anywhere else.

Our trainer wanted us to find out why that was.

The initial and obvious assumption was that I had simply been managing my team better than everyone else had been. I was obviously a fan of this assumption. So we discussed what I had been doing in detail. Were my one-on-ones better? Was I giving better feedback? Was I more consistent and dependable? Was I a better coach?

As it turned out, no. Upsettingly, it didn't seem like I'd been a better manager at all. In fact, it actually seemed more like the opposite was probably true. It really seemed like I might have been a much worse manager than any of my colleagues. I had been incredibly inconsistent with almost everything. I'd made commitments then forgotten about them, I'd randomly changed my mind about stuff I'd wanted done, I'd cancelled one-on-ones with five minutes notice because I'd had other stuff to do. The one-on-one meetings I had done were often shambolic and awkward, and my coaching sessions had usually turned into me just telling people what to do. I had really not even been a good manager, let alone a great one. So it made no sense that people in my department felt so much more valued than anywhere else.

I don't remember how long we spoke about it for, but it was a long time. We covered everything, but couldn't get to the bottom of it. There didn't seem to be a single thing that I had done better than anyone else. We were all getting pretty exasperated trying to work it out, when something occurred to me...

Did the other managers actually care about their people?

I asked them that question, and I saw immediately from the looks on their faces that they didn't. I realised something that day that shaped my entire management career. The tools we are given as managers - the one-on-ones, the communication models, the active listening techniques - these are all tools to make people feel valued and cared about. But people aren't stupid, and if you don't actually care about them, these are just tricks. They won't work.

The reason my team felt valued despite me being an objectively bad manager was simply that I actually did value them. Genuinely. I trusted them, and I wanted all of them to be happy. It was important to me. I viewed it as my job to help them get the most out of work. When I messed up I apologised, not because I was supposed to, but because I was actually sorry. When they did well I was happy, not because I benefited from it, but because they did. When they were struggling I worried for them, not because of the results, but because of how it affected them as people. I wanted the best for them. I really genuinely did.

And it turned out they just knew, they could feel it, because they were human beings. It didn't matter that I messed up the management stuff. They could just see it in my face and hear it in my voice that I was someone that was trying to have their back. Even if I sucked at it. We know when someone cares about us, and we know when someone doesn't. My team all knew I cared, so they forgave me for my near constant mistakes as a manager. When the survey came around they didn't think about the times I'd let them down accidentally or had made mistakes that made their jobs harder. They just thought about the fact that I had in my own flawed way always tried to look out for them, and that's what turned out to matter to them.

I'm glad I have all the management tools I have at my disposal. I believe all managers should learn them and that they are incredibly valuable. But when it comes right down to it, if you care about your people - genuinely care about them - that will shine through even if you make a mess of the management activities a lot of the time. Learn all the management skills, get as good at them as you can be because they help you do the right things at the right time. But if you don't care about your people, none of it will matter.

I created Minimum Effective Management because I know work can be better for everyone, and I know as managers we can really make a difference to people's lives. I created it because I could feel that there was an easier way to get this job done that would be better for the managers and the employees. When I have explained this approach, I am yet to find a single person who doesn't believe they would thrive if they were given this kind of freedom at work by their manager.

So ask yourself this. If you would thrive if given this freedom, why wouldn't your employees?

AFTERWORD

There is a somewhat satisfying parallel between how I came to write this book, and how I came to be a manager in the first place. I actually never intended to have this career. I thought I was going to be a tech person of some sort. My first management role was one I took on reluctantly. At the time, I was working in an IT support department that was a complete mess, and I used to spend the majority of my time moaning about how terrible I thought everything was. I had no intention of actually fixing anything myself though, I just wanted someone else to do it. Eventually, the owner of the company became sick of hearing my constant complaining, and instead of firing me like I expected him to, he told me to shut up and fix things. In fact, as I remember it, my options were to either become the manager of the department, or leave the company entirely. I guess he figured that either way, he wouldn't have to listen to me bitching anymore.

I didn't want to do it. I really didn't want to be a manager. I didn't think I'd be good at it, and I didn't want to be anyone's boss. I'm an extremely introverted person and the idea of a role that made me a focal point was terrifying to me. But there was this part of me, this small but deafeningly loud and persistent part of me, that felt completely certain I could fix things and desperately needed to try. That part of me could see the problems so clearly, and that part of me knew I could make things better. When it came down it, I just couldn't walk away. That part of me wouldn't allow it. So I took the job, and I went into it feeling a strange combination of utter self-doubt, and complete self-belief. I was sure I knew how to fix those problems, I just didn't know if I was the right person to do it.

I found myself feeling the same way about this book. I had no strong desire to write a book. I have always enjoyed writing, but never fancied myself as an author. But this management problem just kept showing itself to me. Every time I would meet up with a friend and they would talk about work, I'd hear the same stories, the same frustration, the same exasperation that they weren't being set free to actually be their best. It would gnaw at me. At first I thought that just fixing it in my own company would be enough for me, but it wasn't. The itch remained unscratched. With each new person that told me about a totally avoidable frustration that they had at work, that voice in my head got louder. That same voice that wanted me to become a manager so I could fix the problems on a small department now wanted me to step up and try to fix the problems with management itself. In the end, in much the same way as when I became a manager, I really didn't have much choice but to write this book. I just had to do it, and I've gone into it with that same mix of utter self-doubt and complete self-belief. I believe completely in this approach, I just hope I was up to the task of explaining it.

RESOURCES

When you strip the administrative tasks away from being a manager by adopting the Minimum Effective Management approach, you're left with a much smaller required skill set. This section provides a brief overview of the key skills any manager needs in order to be effective, no matter which approach they use. There's nothing too in-depth, just the key points of some of the models and approaches that I still use from my traditional management days.

Coaching

When people think of coaching, they often imagine a formal coaching session that's planned and structured. Whilst these sessions can be valuable, I think the majority of the benefit you can get from coaching is during what I guess could be called micro-coaching sessions. That is, the small everyday interactions you have with people when they have problems or ask for your input.

Obviously when someone owns a piece of work in a Minimum Effective Management workplace, they will be responsible for making the decisions relating to that piece of work. This makes coaching vital, because coaching gives you a tool to help them make their decisions in a structured and logical way.

Before I explain the model, I want to expand on some reasons we should try to avoid making decisions for people or giving them specific advice, even if they've come to us for help.

When one of our people tells us they have a problem with something, it's extremely common for us to think we're supposed to give them advice. We'll ask a few questions, think we've got a handle on the situation, then give our suggestions. This isn't good management.

In these situations, think about how much time you will

have had to consider the problem compared to how much time they will have had. The employee will have' been working on this problem for a while before talking to you, whereas you will have only just heard about it. They will have had much more time to consider things than you will have. Even if you believe you're much smarter than they are, are you so much smarter than them that you can make better decisions than they can with just a fraction of the time to think about it? The 10 minute conversation you have with them is not going to catch you up to their level of understanding of the issue at hand. The way you can help them isn't with advice, it's with questions. It's by helping them structure their own thoughts.

The moment you give advice, you create a new set of problems. Let's say you make a suggestion, and they go back and start to work on the solution that you've suggested. If things don't go well, they might feel uncomfortable about changing course because it would mean they were going against what they perceived to be your instructions. You have role power when you're someone's manager, so your suggestions can accidentally carry more weight than you intend them to. It's really common for employees who've been given advice by their manager to follow that advice even if they don't agree with it.

When you give them advice, nobody really wins. If you end up being right, they won't feel a sense of accomplishment because they'll feel like you solved the problem. They also won't learn how you solved the problem because you just gave them the answer, so that means they'll come to you next time they have a problem as well. Alternatively, if you end up being wrong, they won't feel the same sense of responsibility either because you're the one who made the call. They might even start to question your judgement, especially if they didn't agree with you in the first place.

This is where coaching comes in. Coaching isn't about giving advice, it's about helping people make their decisions in a structured and logical way, and it's especially important with Minimum Effective Management. When you work this way, you have inverted the role power, and you are no longer the decision maker. You are there to offer guidance, but ultimately what they do is up to them, so you need to be able to help them make decisions based on a logical approach. You can't get away with just telling them the right thing to do - you have to help them see what the right thing to do is.

The GROW performance coaching model helps you do just that.

GOAL - WHAT IT IS THEY'RE TRYING TO ACHIEVE
What difference do you want to make?
What do you want to achieve?
What do you want to improve?
When do you want to have achieved it by?
How achievable do you think it is?

REALITY - WHAT THE CURRENT SITUATION IS
What are your concerns?
How concerned are you?
Who is affected by this issue?
What have you done already?
What is stopping you at the moment?
What help do you need?
How confident are you that you can do this?

OPTIONS - WAYS TO REACH THE GOAL
What have you already ruled out and why?
What could you do?
Could anyone else help?

Where could you get more information?
What tasks could you delegate?
Is there anything you can do today that would definitely help?

WAY - WHAT THEY'RE ACTUALLY GOING TO DO
What are you going to do?
What support do you need?
Who are you going to get to help you?
How can I help you?
What are you going to do first?
How confident are you that this will get done?
When will you have done this?

The questions I've included for each step are obviously just examples. In terms of execution, I think the model is fairly self-explanatory. You take each step one at a time. You find out where they need to be, where they currently are, and what they could do to bridge the gap. You ask them to examine and explain each option, ask them questions to help them determine which ones are viable or not, and then finally ask them to make a decision on what they're going to do.

What this model does is show you a sensible way to make a decision, and gives you a mechanism to walk someone else through making a sensible decision of their own. You don't have to give advice, you can just ask questions such as the examples included. At the end of the conversation you should have helped them make the best decision they could.

Working this way is the exact opposite of giving advice in terms of the outcome it creates. All the negatives of giving advice become positives here. If they end up making the right choice, they feel a sense of pride and accomplishment. If they end up getting it wrong they feel responsible, but they know they had your support so they don't worry that you will think they messed up. And you know they made the decision logically so you don't feel the need to get more involved next time even though things didn't go the way you'd both hoped.

Most importantly though, you'll find that the more you work like this, the less your people will need you. When you give advice when someone asks for it, they become dependent on your advice. When you help them make a decision rationally, they start to think that way on their own. After a while, people will automatically start thinking this way when they're faced with problems, so you're helping them improve rather than just giving them answers.

The more practise you have at this, and the more your people get used to you doing it, the better your results will be. There's an interaction I'll often have with someone just as we've started to get used to working with one another other...

"Hey Matt, I've got a problem with this, what should I do?"

"I don't know, what should you do?"

If they smile when I say that, I know that we're getting somewhere. It means they've been through the conversation with me enough times to know all the things I usually would have asked before that question, and they can just ask themselves those questions.

Managing performance

The key to effective performance management is understanding the components of performance and identifying which one needs attention.

There's an acronym you can use to help remember these components (it's the only business acronym I actually like). If someone is performing badly, ask yourself: Why do they SUCK?

- Skills
- Understanding
- Competence
- Knowledge

Performance isn't one thing, it's actually four things, and if you address the wrong one, you won't get anywhere. To explain this, I'm going to use tennis again (Bizarrely, I don't even play tennis. I don't know why I'm bringing it up so much).

Let's say you're a tennis coach, and you are working with a player to try to help him win more games.

He has been playing for a few months. He knows all the rules of tennis, and can hit most of the strokes. His serve is terrible though, and he loses most matches because of it. He does everything wrong, his action is all off, and it's horrible to look at.

How do you help him?

Do you tell him what he should be trying to do?

No. He doesn't have a knowledge problem. Explaining to him that he should try to get the ball over the net and into the box on the other side would not be helpful. He knows that's what he's supposed to do.

Do you tell him why it's important he does it?

No. He doesn't have an understanding problem. He is well aware that the reason he is losing games is that he can't win his serve. Giving him this feedback would not help him. He knows it's important he gets better at serving.

Do you ask him to practice on his own?

No. He doesn't have a competence problem. This isn't a skill he has that he just needs to work on. He actually can't do this thing. Asking him to practise the movement wouldn't help him, because he'd be practising doing it wrong.

Should you train him specifically how to serve?

Yes. He does have a skills problem. Time spent with him showing him how to serve properly, breaking down the mechanics of the movement, and adjusting the way he serves would help him win more games. After this, he could practise and work on his competence.

Now let's say you have another player. He has been playing for a little while longer, and his serve is excellent. But not consistently. He is capable of serving well, but not always.

Ask the same questions, and you'll see that even though the problem itself is the same - they are both losing because of their serve - the action you need to take to remedy it is totally different. This player has a competence issue, and his problem isn't actually the serve itself. Showing this guy how to serve would be ineffectual in this case.

When we identify which specific element of performance is the issue, it allows us to make better decisions on how to address it. Being clear on why someone isn't performing is the key to improving their performance. If you try to address one element of performance with the wrong tool, it will be useless at best, counterproductive at worst.

Make sure you know which area of performance you need to focus on before you take any actions to address it.

Giving feedback

Giving Feedback is one of the most important tools available to a manager. It's also one of the most underused. The majority of employees say they don't get enough feedback, and the reason for this is that the majority of managers say they're uncomfortable giving it.

Unfortunately, on the flip-side of this, the managers that are comfortable giving it often give it the wrong way and at the wrong times. There are few things more infuriating than a manager who constantly tells you things you already know, or who criticises you just to make themselves feel better about something going wrong. Striking the balance is important.

Why do you give feedback?

This might seem obvious, but not understanding this is one of the most common problems when it comes to giving feedback. There are only two reasons to give feedback:

- You want to change a behaviour
- You want to ensure a behaviour continues

A lot of managers fall into the trap of thinking they are giving feedback when actually they are just criticising or complaining. The moment you consider giving someone feedback, stop and consider two things:

- Do they know what you're going to tell them already?

- Will telling them make anything better?

Let's look at a quick and extremely mundane example. You have asked one of your team, Mark, to write and send an email to all your key clients. He did this promptly, but after sending it he noticed that it contained a few typos. He's told you about it himself, he knows he made a mistake, and he's annoyed with himself. He tells you he normally gets important emails like that proofread before he sends them, it just slipped his mind this time.

So, should you give Mark feedback?

No. He is already aware he made a mistake. He's upset with himself about it. He already said he usually proofreads them so there's nothing useful you can tell him, He obviously knows that it's bad to send an email with typos in it, or he wouldn't be telling you about it. Any feedback you give him here will not give him any information he doesn't already have. In this case, giving Mark feedback wouldn't just not make things better, it would make things worse. Mark came to you and told you that he made a mistake, if you now explain to him why the mistake he made is bad, it's not going to make him any less likely to repeat it. He knows already. More likely than not when the two of you separate he's going to be muttering unpleasant things about you. He'll be annoyed with himself for making a mistake, and when you tell him what he already knows, he'll direct that anger at you.

Now, let's imagine a slightly different version of this scenario. The same thing has happened, but this time someone else noticed it. You overheard them telling Mark about it, and he didn't seem to think that it mattered that much.

- Does he know what you're going to tell him already?
- Will telling him make anything better?

In this scenario, there is almost certainly a need to give Mark feedback. There's a good chance he doesn't realise it's important not to repeat the mistake, and therefore giving him feedback might mean it's less likely that he will repeat it.

When do you give feedback?

Generally speaking, we need to give feedback the moment we see a specific behaviour we want to change. I heard an expression recently that is very relevant when it comes to feedback: "We encourage what we tolerate". In my experience, if you observe a behaviour and you don't say anything at the time, you've kind of given them feedback already. You've told them what they did was ok. If you're my boss, and you see me do something and you don't say anything, I will assume you're ok with me doing it. If you then come back to me later and tell me you actually weren't happy with it, that's much more likely to get a bad reaction out of me.

That's not to say you can't give feedback on something that happened a while ago, especially if it's something that you have only just found out about. Just try to avoid seeing something and then waiting to talk about it another time.

One belief some managers have that makes them wait to give feedback is that it needs to be given in private. That's not necessarily true. Giving feedback in public shouldn't be a problem. In fact, if you feel like you can't give feedback in public, it's a good indication that you're not delivering it well. Feedback should never be a telling off. It's ludicrous to assume that people could know the perfect way to behave without receiving feedback, so it would be equally ludicrous to treat that feedback as a negative. It should be no more of a negative experience than turning a steering wheel on a car would be. It shouldn't be something you need to do in private. If you make a big deal of doing it in private, you're arguably sending the message that they've done something they should be embarrassed about. Obviously use your judgement, but as a general rule, there's no need to give feedback in private.

One thing to consider regarding when you give feedback though is the medium you use to do it. Sometimes a manager will find out about something, then give someone feedback over email or Slack. Don't ever do this. They need to hear your voice, and you need to be able to discuss things. Even if doing it in person or over a call or hangout would mean doing it later, that's a price worth paying. There are potentially some exceptions to this - such as if you have an exceptionally strong relationship with someone or you're confident there is no chance they'll react badly to what you have to say - but I honestly think it's just not worth the risk. Handling it in a real conversation gives you the best chance of a positive outcome.

How do you give adjusting feedback?
When we want to change a behaviour, we use adjusting feedback. The model I recommend for adjusting feedback has the following three steps:

- Ask if you can give the feedback

- Explain the situation, behaviour, and impact

- Agree a different future behaviour

Ask

This step is so often missed off, but it's the most important one. Taking this step will give you a far better chance of achieving the thing you want, which is changing the behaviour.

Let's go back to our situation with Mark. You just overheard him being told about his mistake, and you noticed that he didn't seem that bothered by it.

Imagine you just go over to him and say, "Mark, sending out an email full of typos makes us look bad". There's nothing too bad about what you've said, but you are coming in a bit hot. There's no time for Mark to get his head right, and as a result there's a chance he may react badly as a kind of snap reaction, and then the tone will be set and it will be hard to change course. People often get defensive when they feel they're being criticised. It's a natural reaction, but there's a simple thing you can do first which can make the whole thing easier. You can ask to give the feedback.

If you say, "Hey Mark, can I give you some feedback about that email?", that gives him a few seconds to switch gears. It means he won't have the snap negative reaction, and by the time he answers you, he'll be ready to listen.

One of the reasons managers often use for not including this step is a worry about giving people the choice. What if they say no - won't that undermine you?

It's actually the complete opposite. When we make mistakes we're often embarrassed and frustrated, and that makes us more likely to get angry with other people. Especially people who point out our mistake. If you just go to Mark and immediately start giving him the feedback before asking him, and he's in the kind of mood where he really doesn't want to hear it, he might very well react badly without thinking. He might argue with you, or just try to brush you off. That actually would be undermining. However, if you ask him if you can give him some feedback and he says no, that's fine. That was an option you gave him. You haven't lost any control. You instigated the exchange by giving him a choice, and he made a choice. It doesn't undermine you at all if he says no. You'd planned for it, and you can just tell him it can wait until later.

And here's the thing. You probably won't have to even talk to him later. He would have known why you wanted to give him the feedback, and he'd have filled in the blanks without you even talking. Just the fact you wanted to talk about it was probably enough. Once he's calmed down he'll probably come to you anyway, and if he doesn't you can talk to him once he's in a better place if you think it's still necessary.

Remember the purpose of the feedback is to change his behaviour. If he's not emotionally ready to listen to you, giving the feedback won't achieve that. So asking if you can give the feedback is always the right choice.

Situation, Behaviour & Impact

You will often see this step broken down to three separate steps. I don't think that's necessarily helpful, as the chances are you're going to do this in one short statement. The shorter you can make this, the better. Otherwise it can feel like a lecture.

Ok, so let's go back to Mark. You've asked him if you can give him some feedback, and he's agreed. What do you do next?

There's a golden rule here that you absolutely must not break: don't say anything that you haven't observed and don't know to be true.

For example, you can't say to Mark:

"You sent an email out to our key clients without proofreading it, and that makes us look unprofessional"

Whilst structurally this is good feedback, there's a problem:

- Do you know Mark didn't proofread it?
- Do you know Mark was even supposed to proofread it? He might have asked someone else to

If you make a statement that isn't true, you're going to end up in a conversation about how that thing didn't actually happen, and it's going to distract from what's really important. The only thing you know is that you asked him to send an email, and that it went out with typos in it. That's what you know, so that's what you can say.

"That email I asked you to send went out with typos in it, and I think that makes us look unprofessional"

If you stick to what's true, there is very little chance Mark can get angry. If you assume anything, you're likely going to get things wrong, and you're going to derail the entire process when you do.

Also notice that you don't have to stick rigidly to the situation, behaviour, impact structure. That's why I think of it as one step. It's clear from that statement what happened, what Mark did, and what the result was. The more rigid you are, the less successful you'll be.

The model is there to show you what information you

need to convey, and you should do that in as few words as possible in language that's natural to you and fits how you usually speak to the person in question.

Future behaviour

This is where you'll see the benefit of only talking about what you know to be true in the previous step.

Let's say you'd made the assumption that Mark hadn't proofread the email, and you'd given him the feedback like this:

> *"You sent an email out to our key clients without proofreading it, and I think that makes us look unprofessional. Can you make sure you proofread it next time please?"*

Again, structurally this feedback is acceptable. Situation, behaviour, impact and new behaviour have all been communicated. But what if you're wrong, and he did proofread it? He'll likely just say, "Yeah, sure", and nothing will improve.

When you don't assume you know anything, you'll realise that you probably need to ask questions before you can agree on a new behaviour. For example:

> *"That email I asked you to send went out with typos in it, and I think that makes us look unprofessional. What happened?"*

Now, let's say Mark explains to you that he did proofread the email, he just did it too quickly and mistakes got past him. Now you have some options?

> *"Are you generally good at proofreading?"*

> *"How do you go about proofreading?"*

"How much time did you spend on proofreading?"

If you haven't assumed you know why the thing happened to begin with, you can have a productive conversation with Mark to get to the bottom of it.

"For important group emails, would it be helpful to get another person to proofread them before they go out?"

"Do you think we need to do something differently to make sure it doesn't happen again?"

Agreeing a new behaviour can almost always be done with questions. You can ask Mark if he thinks anything needs to change, and again, it's fine if he says it doesn't. If he says that it was just a one-time mistake and that nothing needs to be done differently, that's great. He's promised he's on top of it. If not, you can agree on a new behaviour together. But either way, the process of giving feedback has not been in any way confrontational or negative. You asked for a conversation about a thing that happened, and you agreed what to do to try to stop it happening again in the future.

How do you give affirming feedback?

It's easy to overlook affirming feedback. but it's extremely important. Just as much as you want to make sure people change the behaviours that you don't want, you also want to make sure the ones you do want happen more often.

You can do this with affirming feedback.

Imagine you have a new starter, and he's in that timid new starter mindset where he isn't talking much and is a bit nervous still. Work is carrying on as usual and conversations are kind of going on around him, but he's not really getting involved in any of them. Mark works in a different team entirely, but he has noticed that the new guy is nervous, so he goes over to say hello and invites him to lunch.

You like that behaviour. That's how you'd like people to treat new starters, and you wish other people had done it too. If you're a controlling manager, you might consider making a rule that directs people to go and be nice to new starters. That's kind of weird though, and it stops it being a nice gesture when people do it and instead turns it into a creepy corporate policy. There's a much simpler and more human way to encourage this behaviour.

Thank Mark.

The next time you're in a situation where the new guy isn't around, go over to Mark and say:

"Hey, I really appreciate you taking the time to welcome the new guy. It's difficult finding good people and it's always worrying for me when they're not settling in. I felt much better knowing he was being taken care of. Thanks!"

If other people hear you say it, that's a bonus. You've given them adjusting feedback by proxy! They know it's a good thing when people do what Mark did, so they're more likely to do that good thing next time themselves.

Notice that the middle of the model is very similar to adjusting feedback:

- Situation
- Behaviour
- Impact

The only difference with affirming feedback is that the first and last steps are just replaced with a thank you. You don't need to ask, and you don't need a new behaviour. Just say thank you, explain why what they did mattered to you, then thank them again.

Remember, every management tool is precisely that - a tool. Nothing more, nothing less. You don't have to use the tool just because you have access to it. Over time, you'll build your relationships to the point where you can instinctively tell how much of the model you need to use when you give Feedback. My DoThings co-founder and I have reached a point where we can just say "You know that thing you did...well it was shit" and that's all we need to do. We know and trust each other enough that the thinking behind the model is implied.

Getting feedback

Getting feedback is one of the most overlooked management skills there is. Our focus is usually on how to give feedback, but getting it is arguably more important.

Most of the time the reason we don't get valuable feedback is that we are behaving in ways that block it happening. A lot of what many of us assume are good leadership behaviours actually prevent people from giving us honest or useful feedback.

Here, we're going to cover the ways you can accidentally prevent yourself from getting feedback, and the things you can do instead.

Your ego is getting in the way

An extremely common and damaging feedback blocking behaviour is related to your ego. It usually plays out a bit like this:

A member of your team comes to you and gives you some feedback. You quickly decide that they've misunderstood something, and that the thing they're pointing out isn't really a problem at all. So you start to explain why what they're raising isn't actually the problem they think it is. This shuts them down completely. You don't learn anything, and they learn not to bother coming to you in future.

What's crucial to understand here is that even if you are right, and they are wrong, handling it this way makes getting feedback in future much harder. If you hear feedback, you must always assume it might be valid, even if your instinct says it's not. I call this method getting in the car.

If you want to direct where a car is going, you need to get in it first. Just crashing headfirst into it because you think it's going the wrong way isn't effective. If you want to influence the driver, you need to be in the car.

When someone comes to you with feedback, their opinion is all you should be interested in. You don't need to give them yours. Even if you're convinced they're wrong, you need to find out why they think what they think and learn as much as you can.

> *"What do you think would happen when…"*
> *"How would that affect…"*
> *"What if…"*
> *"What do you think that could mean…"*
> *"Why do you think that happens…"*
> *"Have you got any suggestions…"*
> *"Why do you think that is?"*
> *"How could we change this?"*
> *"Who needs to be involved?"*

If you have a proper discussion with people when they give you feedback - even if at the end of the discussion you still don't agree with them - they'll feel like you value their opinion and they'll be more likely to come to you again in future. If you just shut them down immediately, you'll probably never get feedback from them again.

You ask without asking

Quite often, this is what an attempt to get feedback looks like:

"How are things going?"
"Fine"
"No problems?"
"No"
"Great"

And you think everything is fine and there are no problems.

If you want to get feedback you have to ask specific open questions. Nobody feels like they're expected to answer the question "How are things going?" honestly. Imagine if people actually did that, it would be awful. We don't answer that question honestly because the question itself implies the person asking doesn't really want to know. If you want to actually get feedback, you need to ask better questions:

"What have you been working on?"
"What's going well with ..."
"What could be better with ..."
"Would you change anything about ..."
"What would make your life easier?"
"What's the worst thing about..."
"What one thing could I do to make your job better?"
"Who have you been working with?"

You don't need any particular agenda when you ask these questions. Just asking them will show that the door really is open, and that you are really interested. Back when I had a boss, when they showed this kind of interest in me I took that as an opening. I realised it meant that they actually wanted to know what I thought, and I found a way to move the conversation to the thing I wanted to say, regardless of what they asked me. The questions themselves are less important than the fact you're asking them to begin with.

You don't like the way they gave it

Having the ability to get feedback from people who are terrible at giving it is really useful. If you're just going to hear the people who are good communicators, you're shutting down a huge number of people.

Throughout my career, I've worked with people who aren't necessarily the best when it comes to expressing their frustration with how things are going. A lot of the time, someone will sit on something for a long time without mentioning it, then eventually blow up. And when they do, it's really common for managers to focus on the fact that they behaved unprofessionally instead of finding out about the situation that led to it.

This isn't to say the unprofessional behaviour should be ignored, but we should separate the issues. We still want the feedback.

When someone has had a work tantrum, before you talk to them about their behaviour, get the information about what caused it. If you dive straight into giving them feedback about how they behaved, they're extremely unlikely to take that on before you've listened to them about the initial cause of their outburst. Handling it this way will stop you getting the feedback, and make the feedback you give less effective. Listen first, talk after. Once they've been heard, you'll have a much better shot at getting through to them anyway.

You're negative about negative

If you treat what you consider to be negative feedback in a negative way, you're just going to stop hearing it. That doesn't mean everything will have magically become better, it will just mean that you've stopped hearing about the things that are wrong.

This behaviour is kind of self-perpetuating. You reject negative comments, then people stop being negative, so you think your positive attitude has stopped people being negative. It almost certainly hasn't. Those negative conversations are still happening, just not with you.

There's also a clear distinction you need to make between negative feedback, and moaning.

- Negative Feedback is when they tell you about a situation they believe needs to change in order for things to get better
- Moaning is when they complain about something that doesn't need to change, or that obviously can't change

If someone is moaning, you should shut that down. Moaners are terrible people to have on teams and if someone constantly moans I believe they should be fired as a matter of urgency. But people who give negative feedback are your most valuable people. They're the people who are smart enough to see there's a problem, and who care enough to bring it up. You want these people on your team.

The message you should be giving your people is that Negative Feedback is the most positive thing anyone can give you. The people who give it should be held up as examples to the group, and you should always be grateful and excited to hear it.

It's worth reiterating this point - they had to be clever enough to see it, and care enough to bring it up - these people are the people who are going to make you successful.

You're overly positive

A lot of leaders make the mistake of thinking they always need to be positive, no matter what. It's so common that The Lego Movie famously mocked the way of thinking with the song Everything is Awesome.

When you are clearly pretending things are better than they are, you make it so much harder for people to approach you with any feedback that challenges that view. You're telling people that you're not really interested in the bad stuff, you just want to act like everything is fine.

If there's stuff that's not great, acknowledging that is fine. Being positive doesn't mean pretending nothing negative even exists, it just means being positive about the prospects of making things better. You don't need to say "Everything is awesome", you can say "Ok, so this isn't great...how are we going to make it awesome?"

You say this...

This specific example always gets a mention from me, because there are so many people I've worked with who've said it, and because there are still so many people who think this is a good thing for a manager to say.

"I don't want problems, I want solutions"

Don't say this. If you say this to people, they're not going to tell you when something is wrong that they can't resolve, and those are precisely the things you do need them to tell you about. Think about how pointless this message is - if they already have a solution, they shouldn't be coming to you, they should just be getting on with it.

You should encourage your people to bring you problems

that they don't have solutions for. Those are the things you need to hear about. Those are the things you can help with.

If you put effort into getting feedback and you ensure you're not engaging in the typical behaviours that block it, you'll find everything else about the job gets easier. You'll get in front of problems and stop them developing into serious issues, and your people will be far more engaged and empowered.

Goal setting with OKRs

Setting goals with Minimum Effective Management is obviously much simpler than it is traditionally. You'll all be working from one set of goals and therefore this isn't a time consuming process. However, there is still a lot of value to be gained from setting the goals you do have as well as possible. OKRs are probably the clearest and most beneficial way to communicate and track a goal.

There are three components to an OKR that perform very different functions. They are:

- Objectives (Provide motivation and excitement)
- Key Results (Provide measures and guidance)
- Initiatives (Provide the specific actions required)

Objectives

Objectives are the simplest bit, but there are still a few mistakes that are commonly made with them. An objective is something that you want to make happen. There are pretty much no other rules for them. They're the target - the tangible change in the world you want everyone to make happen, however big or small.

- Become the market leader
- Make our customers love us
- Get rich!

All three of these are acceptable objectives. If you're from a

SMART objective background, they will probably seem woefully inadequate, because they're not trying to do as much as a SMART objective would. With SMART, the objective does all the heavy lifting. It communicates what you're trying to achieve, how you'll know you've achieved it, and when you'll have achieved it by. Consequently, they can be a bit uninspiring: Achieve revenue of x by the end of Q4 is not as interesting as Get Rich!, even if it is much more specific.

The primary purpose of an objective is to get people enthusiastic. When my co-founders and I first started DoThings, we had a simple objective: *Get Paid*. We were bootstrapping, so the business wouldn't be able to pay us until it generated revenue. If we'd been using SMART, we'd have had to set a bunch of objectives relating to revenue, expenditure and growth. The resulting objectives would have been correct, but also dull and uninspiring, and they'd have failed to convey the thing we actually wanted, which was for our business to support us financially.

That term I just used, "our business to support us financially", leads me to the next point about objectives. They can be worded however you like, and they work best when they're worded exactly as you would think them or talk about them. The reason our objective was "Get Paid" and not the more professional sounding "Enable our business to support us financially" was that we wanted to word it the way we thought about it. When we were working our asses off building the business, we didn't think to ourselves "won't it be great when the business is able to support us financially". We thought "I can't wait until we can get paid". Wording your objectives the way you think them is really powerful. It makes them more human, and ultimately the more human the objective is, the more effective it will be.

The objective just needs to provide the aspiration. By itself it needn't do anything more than that, but it should do that one thing extremely well. It should be something that people can really get behind and that they'll want to help achieve.

That said, obviously just providing an aspiration isn't going to be enough on its own. You'll need to be able to measure your progress towards it. This is where Key Results come in.

Key Results

Key Results are how you can measure the progress towards your objective. In my experience, this is where the wheels start to fall off for a lot of people. For the sake of clarity we'll only use one Key Result per objective in these examples, but in practice you can set anywhere up to around five.

Let's start with the basics. Key Results must be measurable, they must be numbers, and their values can't be subjective. If the objective component is all about excitement and motivation, Key Results are about measuring and guiding.

John Doeer, one of the leading voices regarding OKRs, uses this formula when setting an OKR:

I will [Objective] as measured by [Key Results]

Misinterpreting this formula is one of the biggest mistakes I see people make when setting OKRs. People often think that this means a Key Result must be a way of measuring if the objective has been achieved. This isn't the case. A Key Result is a way to measure progress, but not necessarily success. This might seem like semantics, but it's a really important distinction.

Imagine you have a simple objective: get a dog. What are the measures of success for if you have a dog or not?

```
Objective: Get a dog
Key Result: Number of dogs to be 1
```

The only measure of success for if you have a dog is the number of dogs you have. Although technically this is still an OKR, in practice it's really not giving you anything useful. The Key Result is completely redundant, but you have nowhere to go if you think of Key Results purely as measures of success.

This is the same objective, but with Key Results being treated as measures of progress:

```
Objective: Get a dog
Key Result: Disposable income over x per
month
```

Obviously your disposable income is not a way for you to measure if you have a dog or not, but it is a way to measure if you can get a dog or not. From this, I can see that the reason I can't have a dog is that I can't afford one, and the thing I need to change to make it possible for me to get a dog is my disposable income.

This is the power of Key Results in comparison to the measures of success that other goal setting frameworks rely on. They can communicate the specific levers that can be pulled in order to get something achieved, even if those things aren't direct measures of success.

None of this is to say that Key Results can't be measures of success - for some objectives that will work perfectly well. They just don't have to be. The important thing for a Key

Result is that it shouldn't be something that can only be measurable in retrospect. If you set the "number of dogs to be 1" Key Result for example, sure, it would be the best measure for if you've achieved the objective or not, but it would offer nothing to you on your way to achieving it.

Another important quality a Key Result should have is that they should be exactly that: Results. Not actions you can take, but the desired results of your actions.

Take this example of an incorrectly set Key Result (taken from a popular OKR example site):

Objective: Hire a Chief Marketing Officer
Key Result: Submit a job listing to 5 major
recruitment platforms

This kind of mistake is extremely common. It's a number, it's quantifiable, so it's an acceptable Key Result, right?

Wrong. This isn't the result of you doing something, this is you doing something. The action itself does not help you achieve your objective. What if you submitted the job listing to five major recruitment platforms, but nobody applied for the role? You wouldn't have made any progress to your objective at all, even though the Key Result was delivered.

A Key Result shouldn't be an action, it should be the intended result of your actions. The way to get this right is to always consider if the Key Result you've chosen is something that actually needs to happen. In the example we're using, posting the job listing wouldn't help you at all unless people applied to the role as a result of it. So, a better Key Result would be:

Objective: Hire a Chief Marketing Officer
Key Result: Receive 20 applications for the
role

To put it simply, a Key Result is exactly what it says it is - it's a result that is key to the success of the objective.

However, what if we still wanted to plan and communicate specific actions that we think will help achieve the Key Result? If we're sure that the best way to receive those 20 applications is to submit the job listing on five major recruitment platforms, how do we communicate that?

We do that with Initiatives.

Initiatives

Initiatives are specific things you can do to affect the Key Results. If it's an action you can take through choice, then it's an Initiative. At DoThings we don't actually call them Initiatives, we call them Projects because it just fits with our natural language more comfortably. Some people call them Deliverables. It doesn't matter what you call them, as long as you understand that they're complete pieces of work you can deliver that you believe will help achieve one or more of your objectives.

```
Objective: Hire a Chief Marketing Officer
Key Result: Receive 20 applications
Initiative: Submit a job listing on all major
recruitment platforms
```

You might be wondering why *Hire a Chief Marketing Officer* isn't an Initiative. After all, isn't that an action you can take? The reason this is an Objective rather than an Initiative comes down to control. Hiring a CMO is not as simple as just doing it. Other things need to happen to allow you to take that action, and it isn't entirely within your control whether it happens or not.

You can't just decide to hire a great CMO. You would first

need to create a role profile, find candidates, create an interview process, carry out interviews etc etc. Hiring a CMO is going to be the end result of a lot of different actions and external factors, rather than an action you can simply carry out the moment you want to do it.

Imagine you were setting OKRs related to getting better at tennis. What category do these three things fall into?

- Win a tournament
- Practise at least five times a week
- Win at least 70% of first serve points

You can simply choose to practise five times a week, so that's an Initiative. It's entirely within your control if that happens or not. However, winning the tournament isn't simply a choice you can make, it's an outcome you want to achieve, so that's an Objective. And something that would make achieving that Objective much more likely is if you were to win at least 70% of your first serve points, so that's a Key Result.

- If it's directly in your control whether it happens or not- it's an Initiative
- If it's the actual thing you want to achieve - it's an Objective
- If it's a measurable outcome that will help you achieve the thing you want to achieve - it's a Key Result

You don't need to decide what your Initiatives are when you're planning your OKRs - in fact, typically with the Minimum Effective Management approach you would make a point of not doing it - but you should keep Initiatives in mind when you're planning in order to make sure you aren't setting Key Results or Objectives that should actually be Initiatives.

Common OKR Questions

How ambitious should objectives be?

This one is really easy. If you ask whoever understands the Objective best if you think it will be achieved, the answer should be "Err...maybe".

The standard guidance is that you should probably be achieving around 60-70% of your OKRs. Any more than that and you're not being ambitious enough, any less and you might want to dial it down a notch. I don't necessarily disagree with that guidance, but I think it's over-complicating it a bit. If you set an Objective and you're not sure if you can achieve it or not, but think you have a good shot, you're probably in the sweet spot.

Objectives should be possible, but far from guaranteed. If you think you'll definitely achieve it, you should aim higher. If you don't think there's any realistic way you can achieve it, you should probably aim lower.

For example, if you're completely convinced you can become one of the market leaders, then maybe you should aim to be *the* market leader. However, if you really don't believe it's possible to become the market leader no matter what you do, maybe you should aim to just become one of the market leaders. Everything should come down to how confident you are at the time.

How often should objectives be set?

This is where I think they are almost always over-complicated. There are various guidelines relating to operational or strategic cadences, and talk of quarterly or annual OKR periods. My advice is to ignore all of this. Respond to what happens in the real world. What's important is what you are trying to achieve, and in most cases those things won't fit into the same neat little time boxes. You don't need to arbitrarily fit all your objectives into set periods. There's no need to have quarterly or annual Objectives, just have Objectives, and set sensible time frames for them on a case by case basis.

- If you want to become the market leading product and you think it will take you two years, then work to that time frame for that Objective
- If you want to move to a new office and you think it will take 13 weeks, set that as the time frame for that Objective
- If you want to become a place people love to work and you think it will take 11 months, set that as the time frame for that Objective

The point is, the time frames should fit your Objectives, not the other way around. When one Objective is complete, you can create a new one. There's no need to do it in batches.

Should OKRs be linked to reward?

This one is more complicated. Coupling bonuses or reward to the success or failure of any OKR is a bad idea. However, this is not the same as coupling reward to results.

Although those two things might sound very similar, they produce very different outcomes. To illustrate this, imagine you want to set this extremely ambitious OKR:

```
Objective: Make our product the market leader
Key Results:
NPS Score over x
Customer Churn below y
Total Customer number over z
```

Now, consider these two ways of approaching reward in relation to this objective.

Bad Approach: Reward Linked to Success

With this approach, you decide to motivate everyone by linking the bonus pool to success or failure of the objective. If you achieve the goal, everyone will get a big bonus. Seems like a good way to motivate everyone to get it achieved, right?

The first problem you're going to face will be immediate. You're going to get pushback on the objective itself. People will say that the goal is too ambitious, because they know there's a good chance they'll fail and that will cost them money. They will want a more realistic objective, and the chances are you're going to have to accept just trying to be one of the market leaders, not the market leader.

The second problem you won't see until later. Imagine there are a couple of months left in the year, and you find yourself in a situation where the objective obviously can't be achieved. Everyone knows they are going to fail no matter what they do, so they stop trying.

Or conversely, you find yourself in a situation where the objective has been achieved with a few months to spare, and with the reward already secured, everyone takes their foot off the pedal.

By linking reward to success or failure, you incentivise

people to set less ambitious goals that are less likely to be achieved or surpassed.

In short, it's not a good idea.

Good Approach: Reward Linked to Metrics

What if instead of linking reward to success of the objective, you link reward to the Total Customer Number metric. You make it so the more paying customers you have, the greater the bonus pool will be (I'm not necessarily advocating this metric or this approach, this is just an example). If you do this:

- Nobody is incentivised to set a less ambitious objective
- There's no reason to give up if it becomes obvious the objective can't be achieved
- There's no reason to stop pushing once the objective is achieved
- You have made it so the staff and the company have aligned financial incentives

Connecting reward to results in this way avoids the problems that connecting to success or failure creates, but still allows you to provide shared economic incentives to succeed. The key word there is *shared*. If the economic incentive for the business is the same as it is for the employees, that's always going to help you. The simple message here is "if we make money, you make money".

I believe this message is extremely powerful - it says the company doesn't expect you to work hard only for the company. It says if we do well, you'll do well too.

Should OKRs be used to evaluate performance?

With the standard application of OKRs, individuals can have their own goals. Obviously with Minimum Effective Management this isn't the case, so the answer in this context is obviously 'No'. When evaluating performance you can look at the OKRs an individual contributed to, but the success or failure of those objectives should be irrelevant. OKRs are not a performance measurement tool, and if you use them that way you'll fall into the same trap as linking them to success or failure for reward. People will push for less ambitious objectives.

Your OKRs are a tool for getting everyone aligned. That's it. You should evaluate individual performance based on job skill, behaviour, and the impact they have on others.

Running one-on-one meetings

When running a one-on-one meeting, there are some simple ground rules you can follow to make sure the meeting is beneficial.

The meeting is for the employee, not the manager

The primary reason you have a one-on-one is to give the employee the chance to talk to their manager. It is their meeting. This means that cancelling the meeting shouldn't be something the manager does just because they don't have anything they need to talk about.

The meeting should be scheduled

When you're still at the stage in your relationship with someone that you feel you need a formal one-on-one, don't just have them on the fly. Schedule them in, keep to the schedule.

The meeting should be structured

You should schedule the meeting for 45 minutes.

- The first 15 minutes should be for the employee to discuss anything they want to discuss
- The second 15 minutes should be for the manager to discuss anything they want to discuss
- The final 15 minutes provides a buffer zone in case either the employee or manager sections over run,

and to allow time to make notes and plan actions that may come out of the meeting

Their time

You should always prepare open questions to ask during the employee's time. Often you'll encounter employees who just say "Um, no I've got nothing to talk about, everything is fine". When this is the case, use their time to ask them about their work, their career, their job satisfaction. Whatever it is, as long it's about them, try to get them talking about themselves in that time period.

Example one-on-one questions:

- How much are you enjoying work?
- What is going well at the moment?
- Why do you think that is?
- What would you like to do more often?
- How satisfied are you with your work?
- What support do you need?
- Do you think you could be utilised more?
- How do you feel you're performing?
- If you could change one thing, what?
- What would be the impact of that?
- Who do you enjoy working with?
- How well do you think the team is functioning?
- Who do you have the least contact with?

Although the meeting is theirs, it's important you don't let it become chaotic. Early on in my career before I'd learned how to control them, some people could turn their one-on-ones into long complaining sessions. But you set the time boundaries for a reason and you should keep to them.

Sometimes people want to talk too much. It's ok to let it happen the first time, it might be a one-off and they might benefit from blowing off steam. However, at the start of your next meeting, set the ground rules at the start. Explain that you went over time last time so you need to keep things more concise this time. Explain that their part of the meeting is 15 minutes, and ask if that's enough time to talk about everything they need to talk about. Assuming it is, if they run over again, cut them off this time. If it's not, you can make a call on extending it on a case by case basis. It's better to agree this up front rather than letting them just ramble for as long as they want to each time you get together.

Your time

Your time can be used for anything you want, and is acceptable for your time to be cut short. If you genuinely don't have anything to say it's better to say nothing than fill this time with stuff that has no value. Your time in the one-on-one is not as crucial as their time.

Aim to make the meetings unnecessary

As I mentioned earlier, all of this thinking now comes with an asterisk. Although one-on-ones are an invaluable tool and every manager should know how to deliver one, I believe your goal with every member of your team should be to develop the relationship to the point where you don't need them. If you are truly close to your people, if they truly trust you and find you approachable, and they know you won't judge them or belittle them or unduly criticise them, then you will probably find they can talk to you whenever they want.

The point of these meetings is to give your people a chance to be heard, and if they're getting that anyway, you don't need the meeting.

About the Author

Matt lives in London with his dog, Business. He briefly joined Twitter, which confirmed his view that the invention of social media was a disaster for humanity. You can now find him absolutely nowhere on the internet

https://dothings.io